"Symbols are the key to communication. Read this fascinating book about self-expression to understand yourself and your ability to change."
> —Bernie Siegel, M.D., author of *Love, Medicine and Miracles* and *Prescriptions for Living*

"Vimala offers a fresh, pure, and striking alphabet to anyone whose handwriting needs some encouragement—even those who are ready to give up. If you clutch and go dismal at the thought of presenting yourself on paper, you need this book."
> —Margaret Shepherd, author of *Calligraphy Made Easy* and *The Art of the Handwritten Note*

"What yoga is to the body-mind, Vimala Rodgers's work is for the mind-body. I highly recommend her joyful book to everyone on the path toward healing and wholeness; it's a missing link in the holistic field."
> —Andrew Ramer, author of *Angel Answers* and *Revelations for a New Millennium*

YOUR HANDWRITING CAN CHANGE YOUR LIFE

VIMALA RODGERS

A FIRESIDE BOOK
Published by Simon & Schuster
New York   London   Sydney   Singapore

FIRESIDE
Rockefeller Center
1230 Avenue of the Americas
New York, NY 10020

FIRESIDE and colophon are registered trademarks
of Simon & Schuster, Inc.

Designed by Bonni Leon-Berman

Manufactured in the United States of America

10   9   8   7   6   5   4   3

Library of Congress Cataloging-in-Publication Data

Rodgers, Vimala.
   Your handwriting can change your life / Vimala Rodgers.
      p. cm.
   "A Fireside book."
   Includes bibliographical references (p.   ) and index.
   1. Graphology.   2. Self-realization.   I. Title.
   BF901.R64 2000
   155.2'82—dc21
                                          99-046322

ISBN 0-684-86541-6 (pbk.)

ACKNOWLEDGMENTS

To Martha & Red Fisher in Mississippi, and Carol & Ralph Meyer in Pennsylvania, I extend an extraordinary thanks for housing me on my sabbatical so this book could be written. A thanks of equal magnitude to my brilliant editor, Marcela Landres, at Simon & Schuster, whose kindly nature unfailingly exudes clarity, directness, honesty, lightheartedness, and understanding—a rare package indeed. I thank you from the bottom of my heart.

CONTENTS

Part One

INTRODUCTION

TO HANDWRITING

ANALYSIS

Chapter 1
WHAT IS HANDWRITING?

The focus of this book is to guide you, the reader, in allowing your hidden gifts, ideas, and abilities to tumble forth—treasures that you tucked away early on. As young children we all developed our own reasons for denying what we really loved to do or for not expressing an idea that no one had heard of before. Innocently sharing it and being greeted with adult ridicule rather than encouragement was often enough to have us quietly stuff those special ideas into a secret place inside—but they don't go away. They merely hide . . . waiting, waiting.

The wall that barricades these special gifts and sabotages our intentions to let them come out of hiding is a simple four-letter word: *fear*. It lives in our mind. We have put it there, and only we can dismantle it and allow our unique gifts to surface.

I can hear your question: "What does my handwriting have to do with all this?" I thought you'd never ask.

HANDWRITING

Our handwriting is far more than a succession of words put together to create a means of communication. It is a map of our attitude toward life, a labyrinthine pathway to long-forgotten hiding places inside, a diagram of our unconscious mind. In simple terms, our writing patterns are clear indicators of how we feel about ourselves. They are a measure of our self-confidence, self-esteem, and self-reliance; they indicate our fears as well as our unique abilities. Self-image is the lens through which we see life, and handwriting patterns mirror the components of the prescription in that lens.

Although the hand—or teeth or toes—holds the pen, it is the brain that causes it to move as it does. When we write, each movement of the pen not only reflects the attitudes we have about ourselves, it reinforces them. Each time we press the pen to the paper to create a letter formation, connect letters, or shape a margin, we are declaring, "This is who I am." The more often we write in a specific manner, the more deeply that attitude is ingrained in our psyche.

Most of us have seen handwriting that caused us to gasp, laugh, or feel a certain way. Signatures especially. At one time or another you may have shown an unknown writer's handwriting or signature to someone and said, "Look at this!" You don't have to be a handwriting expert to gain insights about people through their writing. Essentially, handwriting is a graphic representation of our interpretation of life, indicating how we feel about ourselves and how this feeling affects our view of those around us.

GRAPHOLOGY

Graphology, also called handwriting analysis, is the science that correlates handwriting patterns with personality traits. Professional graphologists are trained in the interpretation of handwriting patterns and their relationship to the personality. Their expertise lies in drawing up a list of personality traits based on a thorough study of a handwriting sample.

GRAPHOTHERAPY

Graphotherapy is the behavioral science that invites the writer to take pen in hand and change self-defeating aspects of the personality by altering specific strokes in the handwriting. Graphotherapists are trained in graphology and have additional training in psychology. Their expertise is to guide the client in altering handwriting patterns as a means of removing negative thought habits and replacing them with positive, self-supportive ones. By changing writing patterns we simultaneously reconfigure the neuropathways in the brain that record our self-image.

WRITING SYSTEMS

I have been fascinated with handwriting patterns since before I could read; as far back as I can remember, the letters of the alphabet have been a special source of intrigue and discovery for me. When as a young teen I took on the study of interpreting handwriting patterns, I ended up doing my own empirical research as I found that most books on graphology were either outdated or did not agree with one another. Through my own studies I discovered that Truth occurs not from belief but only through experience.

From studying pictures of scratchings on ancient cave walls to papyrus rolls and mysterious alphabetical etchings such as Ugaritic script, Akkadian cuneiform, Linear A, and Linear B, my interest in handwriting gained momentum. As I investigated writing systems and phonetic alphabets from around the world I became intrigued at the cross-cultural patterns among them. I found that it was not just the Hebrew or Greek Cabala or the Germanic runes that ordained a special meaning to each alphabetical letter, but that countless traditions around the world did the same thing; the Roman alphabet was no exception.

Then there is Sanskrit. The more deeply I study this incredible language, the foundation of all Indo-European languages, the more spellbound I become by the ancient alphabet in which it is written called *Devanagari* or *script of the gods*. The Sanskrit language itself, known as *Devavani* or *language of the gods,* is not only a deep well of spiritual knowledge, it is also mathematically and tonally precise.

For now, however, the Roman alphabet remains my touchstone, for it is an amazingly rich acculturation of numerous traditions. Besides, I am passionately in love with the English language.

THE VIMALA ALPHABET

In my freshman year of college I took the required Logic course, memorized all of Aristotle's syllogisms, and came up with a personal vision based on conclusions predicated on a modified syllogism of my own. Here it is:

> Since each stroke of the pen reaffirms a thinking habit, and each thinking habit shapes our self-image, and self-image is the lens through which we see life, and this lens determines our behavior . . . if an alphabet were designed that exhibited only the most noble human traits, world peace might be a possibility.

Ah, the visionary mind of a teen! At the time I had no concept of the research or time a project such as this would involve, nor could I envision the joy it would provide along the way.

It has taken me well over thirty years of researching, designing, and refining to accomplish my goal. The end result is The Vimala Alphabet. It is the only writing system that uses handwriting not only as a means of communication but also as a character-building tool, for the shape of each letter reaffirms the writer's most noble qualities. By the mere act of moving the pen across the paper using this alphabet as a model, the writer, on a subconscious level, reaffirms the aspects each letter represents.

Each stroke of The Vimala Alphabet supports the child of God who lives within us all, the child who has a hearty sense of self-esteem, gutsy self-confidence, vigorous curiosity, positive outlook, intrepid creativity, the wisdom of innocence, rampant tolerance, and clear communication skills.

When children use this writing system they establish a repertoire of value-based thinking habits. When adults write these letters they uncover long-hidden abilities and generate the self-confidence to begin expressing them. Turn the page to see what the alphabet looks like.

The Vimala Alphabet

Aa Oo Ðdd Ggg Qq Pp
Yy UUu WwWw Vv
MMm N Nn Hh
LLl EEee Ii JJj
Ff Rrr Ss
TT Kk Bb
Cc Xx
ZZz

1 2 3 4 5 6 7 8 9 0
[ ] " ` ? ¿ * ¡ ! @ # $ % & ( )
+ = - £ ¢ ¶ • – — ∴ ∵
sh s̄ c̄ Th th st sch

As you read Part Two, this particular ordering of the letters will become clear.

Chapter 2
QUESTIONS & ANSWERS

Now that you have seen the letters of the alphabet, let me answer the questions I hear most often.

Q If I write *The Vimala Alphabet*, won't I end up being just like Vimala?

A Absolutely not. You will actually be more authentically yourself. *The Vimala Alphabet* is a template, a guideline.

If you want to be a prima ballerina, first you must take lessons. You must master the exact way to position your feet, to hold your hands, to posture your body, and to tilt your head—all exactly, no guesswork allowed. You must be able to stand and move with precision and grace.

Once you are adept at synchronizing all these difficult maneuvers so they flow in a manner that appears effortless, your own style begins to enter into the dance. No two prima ballerinas dance quite the same; no danseuse leaps, holds, or assumes quite the same attitude. The individuality comes only after years of practice, practice, practice, dedication, and hard work.

Learning healthy handwriting has the same requirements; it also gives breathtaking results, although it takes months rather than years to have them become a part of your psyche and flow automatically.

Q   What will my handwriting end up looking like?

A   The end result of practicing *The Vimala Alphabet* is a relaxed, gentle writing that is simple and clear, easy to read, and a reflection of your unique self. Only you know who that is. Pick up your pen and find out!

Q   Since you stress handwriting so much, why did you have a computer font created?

A   I had *The Vimala Alphabet* digitized into a computer font for three reasons:

1. I'm a realist; I know that many people will never pick up a pen. For those persons, a simple computer font allows them at least to *see* what healthy handwriting looks like. Who knows? Maybe one day— when no one's looking—they'll pick up a pen and give it a go. You just never know; I lay great trust in curious minds.

2. For those who want to write but were devastated by attempting traditional writing systems—or never learned to write script in the first place—*The Vimala Alphabet* is a guiding light. A computer font makes a computer printout available at their fingertips, for persons of any age. They can practice in the privacy of their home, at work, or whenever else they are so inclined.

3. *The Vimala Alphabet* font is my gift to teachers of elementary school through high school. The most common complaint I hear from teachers is, "My students' writing is so illegible, half the time I can't even read their names. And their homework? Hopeless!" *The Vimala Alphabet* is a writing system that flows naturally from the fingertips even for those who have never written before, or who have been intimidated by "penmanship" in school. In other words, it's easy and natural to do.

Teachers can use the font to create and print out their own class materials focused on a self-designed lesson plan, one that is relevant to their particular student population. One of our Vimala Rodgers Institute of Integral Handwriting Studies (IIHS) alumni has been a teacher of English as a Second Language and Literacy classes for more than fifteen years. She has included *The Vimala Alphabet*—handwritten—in her curriculum for years now. Having a font allowed her to include it in her most recent book.*

Q   When we're growing up, why do we change our writing?

A   I often hear comments similar to this: "When I was sixteen I decided to write my S and L just like my best friend Margaret wrote hers. It took a while but then it became easy." My first question would be, "Why the S and L? I wonder why you didn't choose the P or R? the A or G?" The answer is simple. The attitudes reflected in the letters S and L were the aspects of your personality that were shifting. You chose those two letters naturally—if indeed you could call it choosing—because your self-image was changing. What really happened is that the mind chose for you, and the pen complied. As we change our attitude about ourselves, our handwriting changes automatically.

Q   But I'd rather print. It's faster, and besides, I've been doing it for years. What benefit would I gain by starting to write with cursive?

A   Switching to printing is a prime example of changing writing habits dramatically. The reason I hear most frequently is, "because nobody can read my writing." This change most often occurs in boys between the ages of eleven and fourteen, that fragile time when

---

Puppies or Poppies?: ESL Bingo by Elizabeth Kuizenga Romijn. Berkeley, CA: Command Performance Language Institute, 1998.

maturity is approaching, hormones are raging, and uncertainty is king. There is a natural sense of defensiveness and a need for self-protection; printing serves that purpose, for printing shields one's vulnerability. It gives the writer a crust, a protective cover. If you're a printer, be sure to read and re-read the section on printing; it can make a tremendous difference in your life. Tremendous.

Q I'm a thirty-seven-year-old woman. When I was about eleven years old I began to make my handwriting really decorative; it stayed that way for years, then gradually it changed. Why?

A Teenage girls often experiment with new and embellished autographs. They replace *i* dots with circles, hearts, or stars, and their writing tends to be roundish and predominantly in the *midzone*. These are all a reflection of steps in the maturing process, an important part of shaping an emerging identity. As we grow up, these changes evolve into a more mature script because our outlook is more seasoned.

Q Other than appearance, why should I change my handwriting?

A Writing habits reflect thinking habits. By making handwriting changes consciously and purposefully—as you will be guided to do in this book—you will be removing handwriting strokes that indicate your own negative judgments and replacing them with those that allow you to move freely in life, creating access to your own unique life purpose. Once we get out of our own way, nothing stands between us and a life that is fulfilling and joyful.

Q How do you know?

A I have guided thousands of persons in altering their handwriting patterns. Those who took on the changes and practiced relentlessly, letting nothing stop them, tapped into hidden abilities far beyond what they could have consciously imagined.

They began to reshape attitudes about who they were, what they could achieve, and what was possible. They left jobs that were a source of ongoing frustration and entered—or created—positions or companies that were fulfilling and of service to others.

They work harder than they ever had in the past, but not one of them considers it "work." What they are doing now makes them happy, is fulfilling, and they wouldn't change positions with anyone in the world. *They are alive!* The comment I have heard again and again is, "For the first time in my life I know I'm doing what I'm supposed to be doing. What a sense of freedom!"

In all the persons I have worked with I have not met one who was afraid of failure. Not one. I have, however, met thousands who were terrified of success. Thousands. Most of us hide our light under a bushel basket, then complain that the light doesn't shine through. If that is you, and you know you are here for a reason but can't quite define it, I offer this book as a path to self-discovery and fulfillment. Reading the information can be educational and exciting; applying it can be life changing.

ANSWERS TO FREQUENTLY ASKED QUESTIONS ABOUT GRAPHOTHERAPY

Q   What's wrong with the way I learned to write?

A   The way most of us learned to write—at least in the United States—was according to the Palmer System. As with all alphabets, it reflects the values of its time; it was created in 1895. If the way you see the world is not in synch with traditional America of the nineteenth century, you simply will not be able to imitate writing patterns that reflect it.

A person who loves tradition, who may collect antiques, embroider, crochet, delve into genealogy, or engage in other activities common around the turn of the century, will tend to write a traditional script naturally. Your handwriting is an undistorted mirror of how you see yourself and the world. It is neither right nor wrong. It is merely how you see.

If you had a difficult time in penmanship class because, try as you may, you simply could not write the way you were being taught, it may have had nothing to do with insufficient motor control or a low degree of intelligence. It just may be that your mind was round and refused to fit in a square hole.

Q What if I take on writing changes, but don't believe they will make a difference?

A Belief has nothing to do with altering thought patterns through changing handwriting. We write the way we do because we think the way we do. Our thought habits are reflected in the neurological patterns in the brain. When we alter the way we write we are simultaneously altering the way we think, and the neuronal pathways shift accordingly. If you adopt specific handwriting changes without knowing what effect they might have, the result would be the same as though you knew ahead of time. It works automatically.

Q What if I like my handwriting just the way it is, and don't want to change it?

A If you are comfortable with your handwriting, then your life must be unfolding just the way you want it to. By keeping your handwriting as it is, your attitude toward life will not change. If that works for you, then don't change your handwriting.

THE FIVE NOBLE TRUTHS OF GRAPHOTHERAPY*

I'd like to preface our journey together with five extremely important concepts. I call them The Five Noble Truths of Graphotherapy. I invite you to refer to them again and again as you use this book. It will help you release judgment of yourself and others and experience both awe and delight in the process of self-discovery. No other journey is quite as thrilling.

1. There is no such thing in either handwriting or people as good, bad, right, or wrong. Those four qualities are merely opinions, and hold no weight whatsoever in working with the precious commodity called Myself. Who you are is who you are. What you do is what you do. Evaluation of either of these is only a matter of personal interpretation, and as such, is without value except to the one who holds on to it.

2. The frequency with which a writing habit occurs in your writing is the frequency with which the quality it represents occurs in your life. If you see certain stroke placements and formations now and again, then the traits they represent occur only now and again in your life. If there are consistently repeated patterns in your writing, there is a direct correlation between them and the consistency with which the traits they represent occur in your life.

* *Change Your Handwriting, Change Your Life* by Vimala Rodgers. Berkeley, CA: Celestial Arts, 1993.

3. In looking at the handwriting of someone with whom you are in a relationship, both your handwriting and the other person's are required if you want to find out how buttons are getting pushed and what is activating them. Remember Noble Truth Number One.

4. The degree of difficulty in the mastery of a stroke change is directly proportional to the value it will have in your life: The greater the difficulty, the greater the value.

5. Once the commitment to claim your wholeness is firmly in place and you begin to alter strokes in your handwriting, you will be given immediate and intimate opportunities to prove your intention. The moment you declare with your pen that you are now willing to complete an issue in your life (let go of negative judgment in some regard) the issue you are dealing with will confront you immediately and clearly, in the form of a person, a situation, or a relationship.

These truths do not vary.

Chapter 3
MAJOR COMPONENTS
OF HANDWRITING

Since this is a going to be a journey, we are going to draw a map and you get to be the mapmaker. Before you read any further, find a piece of *unlined* 8½-by-11-inch sheet of paper, a hard surface on which to write (such as a tabletop), and a ballpoint pen. Use a ballpoint pen because it gives more information about handwriting than any other type of writing implement. Above all, do not use pencil, felt-tip pen, or Rollerball for the purpose of this exercise. I will explain the implications later on. Now fill the page with your writing.

As you write, use your own words. Don't quote anybody, don't copy from a brochure or newspaper. Write about something that stirs you positively or negatively: abortion, animal rights, the National Rifle Association, the environment, downtown parking.

Choose a topic that will cause the pen to move rapidly. Make sure there are no lines on or behind the paper. Write freely and quickly. No one is going to see this but you, so don't worry about spelling, punctuation, or being profound. Once you have finished writing, sign your name. Now, get another blank sheet of paper, also unlined, and put it next to the paper you just filled.

CAUTION!

Before we go on, I want to share with you the two most important concepts to keep in mind as you begin studying your handwriting patterns, for without them you will become judge and jury, and your verdict will be unfounded.

1. Virtually all writing patterns have both a negative and positive implication. In some instances a loop, a curve, an angle may have a positive connotation; in others, the same kind of loop, curve, or angle may be negative. This is true of 95 percent of all handwriting strokes.

2. Because all handwriting traits are closely interlinked, like cells in a body, each one must be considered in order to create a composite of the entire personality. One handwriting trait is not the whole personality, it is only one piece.

When I speak to large groups I bring a tapestry bag filled with the pieces of a 10,000-piece jigsaw puzzle. I pass the bag around with this request: "Without looking, please choose one—only one—piece of this puzzle, and put it facedown in your hand. Do not look at the colored side until everyone has a piece.

"Now turn over your puzzle piece and look at it for ten seconds. Do not look at your neighbors', only at yours. Study it carefully. Now look up. If any of you can describe the entire puzzle from the piece you are holding, this is yours." At that point I hold up a crisp $100 bill. In twelve years of speaking, I have not yet given that bill away.

I invite you to keep this visual in front of you as you begin to map out your future. Think of your personality as a vast jigsaw puzzle. Each piece is valuable in making the picture complete—but still, it is only one piece.

MAPPING IT OUT

The piece of paper on which we write is like a blank canvas of how we live our lives. As we fill up the paper, so we fill up our lives.

Observing your writing, use the blank sheet of paper to write down your answers to the following questions:

1. Do you prefer to use lined or unlined paper?

2. Which way do you *turn the paper?* Landscape ☐ or portrait ☐?

3. Do you fill up the entire page or do you leave space around the edges? Which edges: right, left, top, or bottom? How much space?

4. Do your lines of writing go straight across the page or do they tend to go uphill or downhill? Now and again, or always?

5. What about the *baseline?* Is it reasonably straight or does it vacillate?

6. On the average, how close are your words to one another? Do they almost touch, is there a space between them, or are they pretty far apart? Or does the spacing vary?

7. Do you finish any strokes in a leftward direction? For instance, crossing a lowercase *t* from right to left?

8. Do you finish any words with *upswings*? *ℓ* If yes, how often?

9. What *size* is your writing? Pretty average or smaller or larger than average?

10. Do you connect each letter within a word, or are some words broken up? How often does this occur? (If you're a printer, just put, "I print.")

11. How much pressure do you put on the pen? Can you feel the writing through the other side of the paper (heavy pressure)? Is your writing moderate with no indentation (average pressure)? Or is it faint on the page (light pressure)?

12. What is your preferred writing implement? Pen? If yes, what kind? Rollerball? Felt tip? Fountain? Ballpoint? Or are you most comfortable using a pencil? If yes, how often do you use it?

13. What about the *slant?* Does your writing lean backward (to the left), forward (to the right), or is it fairly straight up and down? Does it change directions regularly?

14. Are your writing zones fairly in balance? In other words, do you have tall upstrokes, long downstrokes, and an average-sized middle zone? If not, which zone predominates?

15. Do you have a lot of *loops* in your writing? Where do most of them occur: in the upper zone, in the midzone, or in the lower zone? If you have few or no loops, put "none."

16. Which are there more of in your writing, *angles* or *curves?* Or is it a balance of the two?

17. Do you print rather than write? If yes, do you use a mixture of uppercase and lowercase letters? Or only uppercase? Or only lowercase?

18. A ligature is a combination of two letters, the second one of which is created from a part of the first one. The *th* is the ligature I want you to look for in your handwriting. It is a stroke that is key to being flexible and open-minded. How many did you find?

19. Describe your autograph. Is it clear and easy to read? Do you circle it or draw through it? Is one name easier to read than the other? Which one? Does your autograph resemble your handwriting? Study the way you write your name. Does it feel like you?

20. Describe the overall look of your writing on the page.

PERSONALIZING YOUR MAP
FOR THE JOURNEY

The handwriting elements highlighted in the previous section are not the only components of handwriting; there are hundreds of thousands. For our purposes, however, they are the core components that can guide you in drawing a map to a destination of your own choosing by removing roadblocks and replacing them with expansive pathways.

Keep in mind that there is no good or bad in handwriting and there are no right or wrong answers. Remember Noble Truth Number One: There is no such thing in either handwriting or people as good, bad, right, or wrong.

We human beings are wired to see ourselves as either right or wrong, good or bad. As we explore your handwriting patterns and your personality I invite you to enter the middle ground, which is value neutral.

The purpose of our journey together is to remove any self-defeating attitudes that prevent you from seeing who you really are underneath it all. You have put these attitudes in place, and now you get to remove them gently, one at a time.

Use my observations as guideposts, not concrete pillars. Be gentle with yourself, appreciate who you are, and draw your map with a loving touch. Get ready for the ride of your life!

Miracle Notes

Taking on handwriting changes is not a haphazard practice; it requires time and commitment. Commitment has a magnetic energy that draws to it what it needs to expand, generating what may appear to some to be the impossible. I label these occurrences miracles. After only a few days of practice they will begin to occur.

Throughout the book I urge you to jot Miracle Notes to yourself. There are two reasons I do this: When life begins to work for us, it is so easy to forget "how it used to be" without a reminder of the daily changes, and I want you to see for yourself that changing your handwriting—aka changing your thinking patterns—is what gave these miracles permission to surface.

Against the background of firm commitment, your daily handwriting practice will cause huge breakthroughs to manifest. Because it's so easy to chalk it up to fate or some other outside source, I want you to see clearly, with no doubt whatsoever, that you triggered the change.

With persons of intent, purpose, and commitment, miracles are a natural result of daily practice. Despite this, I cannot count how many clients I have had who have practiced rigorously each day— people who have developed a new awareness of their handwriting with every movement of the pen, who have taken on every assignment I have given them and have had life-changing breakthroughs in their lives—and then call to ask, "But Vimala, these things might have happened anyway. How do you know the handwriting had anything to do with it?"

Years ago I expressed my disbelief that they could even entertain such a doubt. My answer would be, "You have to be joking! As hard as you've worked? The life changes you've experienced had *everything* to do with your handwriting changes."

A little wiser and far more accustomed to hearing the question, my answer through the years has changed. Now I reply, "If you want to find out whether or not it was your handwriting that made the difference, why don't you go back to writing the way you used to write and see what happens?" To date, no one has taken me up on that offer. The miracles continue to abound.

1. Lined or Unlined Paper

When you write, you are designing your life, just as an artist paints a picture. Would an artist paint on a lined canvas? The use of lines reaffirms the need to follow along with the prevailing structure, make few waves, color inside the lines, rock no one's boat, and be right. People who must have lines often feel physically ill when, for one reason or another, they must write on unlined paper. It is as though their security has been pulled away from them and their mind frantically gropes for it. You can almost hear them screaming, "Who took my lines? Where are my lines? Give me my lines!"

The one group of professionals with whom I most often work are engineers. I find their logical minds a delight. They are often affronted, however, when I hand out lined paper and ask them to put aside their grid paper for the duration of my presentation. A few minutes after the grumbling has subsided I ask them to put aside the lined paper and I give them unlined paper.

Eyes glaze over, bodies tighten, and the fear is palpable. It's not uncommon for people to start looking around for the exit door. Once the paper is handed out, I make a request: "Now pick up your pen and write five or six lines about anything that comes to mind." I do not exaggerate when I say that beads of perspiration begin to form on the foreheads of many of those present.

At this point I stop. "Look around the room and remember: all I'm talking about is a pen and a piece of unlined paper. You'd think I had asked you to walk blindfolded across a minefield!" In a flash, everyone gets what is happening and we all have a good laugh. Then they begin hesitantly to write, exchanging laughter and murmurs as they move their pens.

Many of those who have a glimmer of a dimension beyond their linear world, and who sense they have a distant dream tucked some-where inside, often take on the No Lines Challenge from that mo-ment on. I have received many letters expressing gratitude for the results of taking on this one writing change.

The letter I prize most highly is from a quiet-spoken software en-gineer in Silicon Valley, who, after he heard me speak, began writing on unlined paper and at the same time began turning his paper in the landscape direction (see number two below). Within seven months he had left his engineering position to begin his own start-up com-pany. Was it only these writing changes that moved him forward? I have no way of knowing, nor has he. I *do* know, however, that he continues to turn his paper "sideways," has never gone back to using lined paper, and has invited his management team to do the same.

If you have a clear, definite preference for using lined paper over unlined and have an idea that just won't take on a concrete form, my recommendation is that you purposefully and consistently use paper without lines for the next two or three weeks and see what happens.

Keep a pad of paper with you; take notes. Notice instances when your thinking loosens up, your creative gears seem to run more smoothly, and ideas seem to drop freely into your mind out of the blue. This would be the natural result of adopting this one writing change. Will it work? Find out for yourself!

2. Direction of the Paper: Portrait or Landscape

Portrait Direction

In school we are accustomed to writing in the portrait direction on binder paper with horizontal blue lines and a red vertical line creat-ing a margin on the left. Because this direction is customary, tradi-tional, and common, most often persons who find it difficult to dance to their own drummer turn their pages in this direction to write. It's familiar. It's safe. It's acceptable. It's usually lined. If not, it has a safe border around it.

If you have a definite preference for writing in the portrait direction, you may find yourself worrying about what others may think should you strike out on your own, creating what they may consider an impossible dream. You may begin to move in a new direction, but then retreat to safe, familiar ground when confronted by obstacles. Writing in the portrait direction supports this kind of restrictive thinking because it inhibits the ability to see things in fresh new ways.

If this sounds like you, begin the habit of turning your unlined paper in the landscape direction when you write, every time you write, even if it's only a shopping list or memo. Think of it as a quantum step toward instilling a good habit that can profoundly affect the direction the rest of your life will be taking.

Landscape Direction

Those who naturally turn their page in the landscape direction are usually the idealists, the dreamers, those who become restless when they are made to follow what everyone else is doing or has done. They tend to think for themselves rather than let others do their thinking for them. They take risks where others might hesitate, and are often pioneers in some field. They are the trailblazers.

I urge you to write in the customary portrait direction in one instance, however: if you use ledger sheets rather than a computer to do your bookkeeping. Too much creative thinking here might cause you problems when it comes time to balance the figures!

If you want to begin thinking "out of the box," however, and discover a fresh new way of looking at your relationships, your job, your attitudes, and create the possibility of turning around self-defeating patterns you keep repeating in your life . . . go landscape.

3. Outer Margins

In handwriting, the spaces created around the edges of the paper are called margins. There are four: upper, lower, left, and right. They each represent something different; how you design them gives specific information about your thought processes.

Upper Margin

Looking at your paper, what does the upper margin look like? Is there quite a bit of space between the top edge of the paper and where the writing begins? Or does the writing start quite near the upper edge of the paper?

Narrow Upper Margin

This particular margin represents your attitude toward authority figures. There are other elements in handwriting that indicate this as well, but the upper margin is a major indicator. The closer to the upper edge of the paper your writing begins, the more resistance you may have toward accepting direction or correction. Julius Caesar, who in his day was considered *Diuus Iulius,* or the Deified Julius, reduced his reports to book form on either a roll or codex and wrote right along the upper edge without allowing any space at all. A healthy *upper margin* on an 8½-by-11-inch sheet is about 1½ inches.

If you consistently begin your writing near the top edge of the paper, when someone asks you to do something you may hear it as an order rather than as a simple request. You may tend to become resentful or annoyed easily. You may feel that other people don't know what they're talking about. You may feel superior to others, above rules and regulations. Your personal relationships may be filled more with confrontation than with lightheartedness and joy.

Like the pieces in a jigsaw puzzle, it takes far more than one handwriting trait to define a personality. I am merely asking you to see if you write this way, then notice if one or more of these attitudes plague you. If they do, start your writing gently away from the top edge of the paper from now on and see how it makes you feel. Remember Noble Truth Number Four: The degree of difficulty in the mastery of a stroke change is directly proportional to the value it will have in your life; the greater the difficulty, the greater the value.

If you're feeling brave and choose to make this change, also begin to use the phrase "I may be wrong" *sincerely* at least twice a day and notice how your relationships with others are impacted. Above all, jot progressive *Miracle Notes* to yourself each day without fail. You may be astounded at what begins to move and shift in your life, especially in personal interactions.

Wide Upper Margin

If you begin your writing more than 2 inches from the top edge of the paper you may find yourself giving in to every request, often letting others steamroll you. If this seems to fit, move your writing up a little, so it is about 1½ inches from the top edge. This will modify an excessive need to please others. It will also diminish the fear of being shouted at.

Narrow Left Margin

Now it's time to look at the left side of the paper, and the left margin. Notice how close to the edge of the paper your writing begins. Because we write from left to right, the left margin represents where we are coming from: the past, home, mom, life as it was when we were growing up. The closer you start your writing to this edge, the more you rely on those memories to create your present.

You may be in a relationship that is similar to—if not just like—your parents'. You may find yourself making decisions springing not from the common sense of the situation or how *you* think, but based on the lifeview of your mother or father, even if it's contrary to your belief system.

You may still be ruminating on your childhood, casting blame hither and yon. You may speak of your past more than most people do, which can be paralyzing, for it takes you out of the present, which is all we really have.

A healthy left margin on an 8½-by-11-inch sheet of paper is about 1 inch in from the edge. It will vary a bit slightly from line to line, but keep it at about one inch.

Wide Left Margin

If your left margin is excessively wide, it may reflect a yanking away from your family of origin without handling your judgments of memories that still cause you pain. Creating an excessively wide left margin is like erecting a massive wall of stone and refusing to believe it's there.

Other handwriting indicators are necessary to verify this, but if it fits, you might want to alter your margin to be about 1 inch and see how your attitudes begin to soften. It's a simple and lovely way to begin letting go of negative thoughts.

Wide Right Margin

Just as the left margin represents where we have come from, the right margin represents where we are going: the future. If your right margin is wide, you are holding the future at bay rather than flowing into it.

For visionaries, dreamers, and people who want to discover who they really are, I recommend you write just as close to the right edge of the paper as you can. English has many words that hyphenate strangely, so the right margin is naturally the most erratic of all.

Narrow Right Margin

Although the ideal is to write as far to the right as possible, it's not a good idea to cram words right up to the edge or to curl them around to fit. This represents a person who disregards boundaries set by others. Just ease the words over naturally. In doing so you are blazing a trail to your future, inviting the unknown and the unexpected.

Lower Margin

This margin represents our aesthetic sense, our appreciation of beauty and elegance: the more generous the margin, the more we value these qualities. It is the most difficult margin to assess because often we begin to write a note using only one piece of paper and as we write we think of more and more things to say. As a result, our writing ends up going to the very bottom of the page, and sometimes up the side! Plan ahead; design this margin as though it were part of the picture you are drawing with your words. Because space is so limited, the lower margin on a postal card doesn't count.

4. Line Direction

The line direction is the slant of the line as your writing goes across the page. Does your handwriting go straight across? tilted slightly upward? tilted slightly downward? What was your answer here?

For obvious reasons, this parameter of handwriting is relevant only when there were no lines on or behind the paper as the writer moved the pen.

Straight Across

Line direction is a clear indicator of the attitude with which you greet life, and your belief in your own ability to achieve. A line that drives across the page as though it were an arrow shot from a bow shows that your are a goal-driven no-nonsense kind of person. When you set a goal you charge after it with attention, drive, and determination, knowing you will get there.

Combining this characteristic with other factors, however, it can also indicate an inflexible attitude, especially if a ruler is used to create a straight baseline, so don't become extreme here. Eyeball your baseline; don't measure it. The easiest way to tell the direction of a baseline is to hold the paper flat, put it about 8 inches from your nose with the lines heading away from you, and glance at it from there. See number five, Baseline, below.

Upward Slope

When your lines consistently slope slightly upward it shows that you have a positive, win-win attitude, and find something beneficial in any situation. It takes a lot to get you down. If you do get discouraged now and again, it doesn't last for long. Note: I said "slightly" upward. An extreme upward sloping line indicates a person who is completely out of touch with reality and covers it up with an artificial "always cheery" attitude. Not surprisingly, any extreme in handwriting reflects an extreme in attitude.

The gently upward-sloping line reflects the writing of a possibility thinker. I have a dear friend whose lines have done this as long as I have known her. Several years ago I asked her this question: "If you were stranded on a desert island and could bring only one book with you, which one would you select?" Because she is such a voracious reader, I assumed she would give this a great deal of thought before answering. Wrong. Within ten seconds her face broke into a huge grin and she responded, "*McDougall's Guide to Ship Building*!" Need I say more?

Downward Slope

The opposite is true of the writer whose lines slope slightly downward. No matter the situation, this writer automatically sees only the negative possibility. If this writer were to win a million dollars, she or he would probably think, "Oh no. Now everyone will want to borrow money from me!" or "Oh well. The government will take most of it in taxes anyway."

A few years ago I had a client who was an accomplished fine artist. Ethel's paintings hung in galleries, she taught watercolor painting to children, and her work was featured in major newspapers and art magazines. When she came to see me I was surprised to see that her handwriting sloped dramatically downward. As I studied the rest of her writing patterns I saw the predicament: She had no faith in herself, her self-image was nonsupportive of her gifts, and emotionally and mentally she was depleted. She had given up. "My work isn't what I want it to be, my career's at a dead end, and so is my life. I don't know what to do" were her opening words.

Because so much negative self-talk was evidenced in her writing, I recommended only one initial writing change. I knew that suggesting more than that might be more than she could presently handle. "Begin journaling every day, writing at least two full pages. Be gentle with yourself. Write slowly, and when you do, direct the baseline of your writing straight across the page." "That's it?" she asked. I laughed. "You may find that it's not as easy as it sounds."

In the next two weeks she faxed her writing to me regularly and called now and again. "I just can't get those lines straight. Try as I may, they keep curving downward!" We would talk for a bit, then she would pick up her pen and begin anew. By the third week her attitude was perceptibly lighter, her voice more lilting, and her lines were, to use her own words, "finally beginning to behave." I didn't hear from her again until our next appointment.

When Ethel came to see me on day forty, it was as though a new person had bounced into my office: same name, same human being, but fueled by a completely different set of attitudes. She had a broad smile on her face, her step was light, and her eyes had a twinkle in them; she was quick to laugh, and had outlined an entire page of how she planned on furthering her career. She persisted with her daily writing practice and it paid off.

A downsloping writing line is a difficult habit to break because the attitude has taken a long time to embed itself in the psyche. It is a major roadblock that, once removed, will have the entire world looking like a different place. Not just pathways, but expressways will open themselves to you once this habit is transformed.

One way to adjust the tendency of downward-sloping lines is always to use unlined paper. Before you begin your writing, make a horizontal crease in the middle of the paper. Flatten out the paper again before you start writing, and as your writing reaches the fold you will be able to tell in which direction your lines are going. If you see that they are tending downward, you can quietly straighten them out.

Above all, do not draw a line across the paper as a guide. When your pen meets a subtle fold it is a gentle reminder; when it meets a line it is a harsh reprimand.

These are fun exercises, not grueling penances. We're just realigning our attitudes, remember? This particular exercise can work wonders in instilling a positive self-image and a forward-looking attitude.

5. Baseline

The baseline is the imaginary line created when you write across the paper. How did you assess yours? Is it reasonably straight or does it create dips and waves as it seems to lurch dizzily forward?

Straight Versus Rigid

A steady-as-you-go baseline is what you want. No extremes here. A baseline that looks as though a ruler were held beneath it indicates rigidity, a fear of being proved wrong, and an obsession with structure—in other words, a writer who imposes overwhelming, self-induced stress on himself and in the lives of those around him.

Wavering Baseline

At the other extreme, a baseline that is hard to follow because it wavers a great deal says that the writer cannot focus in any one direction for very long. Creating a to-do list would generate maximum stress, and life goals would be a laughable impossibility. There are many other indicators that show this, but the baseline is a key indicator.

Any extreme in handwriting will hold us back from being balanced. The ideal baseline is reasonably straight—neither rigid nor wobbly. If yours is way off in one direction or another, you might want to make every effort to balance it. It will do wonders toward bringing a sense of ease into your life.

6. Word Spacing

How did you score on this one? It's a hard call because words often vary in their spacing to one another. What we are looking for again is no extremes.

The ideal spacing between words is the width of a horizontally expanded oval, lowercase *a*. Horizontally expanded means neither compressed nor completely round, but somewhere gently between the two.

Spacing between words indicates your attitude toward socializing, of needing to have people around. Think of words as people. How close you space them indicates how close you want them to you.

Hold your paper at arm's length to get an overall view of how close or far apart your words generally are. If they are extraordinarily close together, you may have a compulsive need to be around people all the time. If they are far apart, you prefer to keep your distance.

Closely Spaced Words

If you find that on the average your words are quite close together, as you practice your writing give them a little more room, a little more breathing space. In doing so with your word placement, you are doing so with yourself.

Widely Spaced Words

If your words look as though they were a cut-and-paste job placed far apart on the page one at a time, gradually begin to bring them closer to one another as you write. Wide word spacing does not say that you are unfriendly; it says that you prefer to define your own space, usually at arm's length.

Moving your words a little closer together will not turn you into a social butterfly; it will simply give you more space in which to relate.

Altering word spacing may sound like a snap, but remember—as you balance the spacing of your words you are simultaneously setting aside your fear of being vulnerable and intimate and choosing to balance your need for interaction with others. This is a deeply ingrained preference, and may take a full forty days to readjust.

Be patient with yourself. Any extreme here is certainly worth removing, especially if you have difficulty creating new relationships and want that one special person by your side, a friend with whom you can let down your hair, be yourself, and who loves you when you do.

7. Direction of Stroke Endings

One of the basics of self-supportive writing is to end as many strokes as possible in a rightward direction. Where a stroke begins indicates where the energy originates. Where it ends indicates where the energy is released. Remember that the left side of the page represents the past, home, your family of origin, and your upbringing; the right side reflects the future and what it is made of. Thus, rightward-ending strokes draw us ahead; leftward-ending strokes propel us backward.

"But what of genealogists, historians, researchers, linguists, and lovers of literature?" you ask. "They dwell in the past." I would have to agree. Their research, however, *originates* in the past, it does not end there; it is self-perpetuating. There are many other strokes in handwriting that indicate a writer who researches and resources the past; ending strokes to the left is not one of them.

Leftward-ending Strokes

Each time a stroke ends to the left it indicates where your attention is being released. If you feel comfortable ending quite a few strokes to the left, your past is coloring your present and thus your future, in brilliant fluorescent shades. You may be looking to the past for approval, you may be repeating the past—especially in relationships—or you may be following a career of your parents' choosing rather than your own. The past affects each of us uniquely.

Many strokes that end in a leftward direction may indicate self-blame, guilt, and a sense of personal inadequacy based on your past. All of them reflect a fear of moving ahead. Left-ending strokes throw you into the past where you ruminate and relive what cannot be undone. They hold you back from experimenting with unfamiliar and perhaps exciting approaches to life. They reaffirm fear and self-doubt, particularly in regard to the motives of others.

Some left-handed writers consider it a natural shortcut to swing the stroke back up and over to the left as a way of crossing their $\mathcal{T}$'s. They look something like this: $\mathcal{D}$. I also see right-handers who have this same habit. It is one writing pattern I urge you to change, no matter which hand you write with.

The future is ahead of you; the past is behind. The direction of stroke endings is a major indicator of which one is shaping your decisions.

8. Upswings as Ending Strokes

An *upswing* is a stroke that curves upward at the end of a word, ascending more that half the height of the final letter. An example is given in number eight under "Mapping It Out" at the beginning of this chapter. When you searched your writing for upswings, did you have to look carefully or were they apparent at a glance? If they jumped off the page at you, I strongly suggest you make it a top priority to change them.

The ideal curved stroke ending goes less than half the height of the letter it is a part of. *a, d, u, m, n, h, e, i, f, r, T* are examples of self-supportive stroke endings.

By its very formation, any upswing blocks forward motion. Again, in life we move from the past to the future—translated into writing patterns, from left to right. When anything blocks forward motion in our writing it is a symbol of placing a barrier in our path. No one else put it there; we alone hold the pen. An example of a barrier may be arrogance, denial, a cavalier attitude, or a closed mind; we design our own barriers uniquely.

The prime ingredient of any mental barrier, no matter how small, is fear, since nothing else holds us back from expressing life fully. Nothing. We can blame circumstances, other people, lack of education, opportunities, or money, but they are not the issues. Fear-based thinking compels us to label these challenges as responsible for our state in life; we then give way to them rather than standing up to confront them.

Upswings are strokes that reflect patterns of deeply ingrained fear. People who write them consistently often find themselves using the same negative phrases in their speaking that their parents used with them.

If upswings occurred only now and again on your page and you weren't even sure if they qualified, simply be aware of them as you write, and nip the tendency now to write them ever again.

If they seem to be everywhere, eliminating them can create a major shift in your thinking habits and in your life. It will give you an enormous assist in breathing deeply and becoming your own person.

It will allow you to let down your guard and open up your life; your interactions with people will loosen up, lighten, and become more effortless. It will give you a sense of freedom unlike any you

may have experienced. If personal freedom and healthy, joy-filled relationships are values you hold dear, I strongly urge you to eliminate
upswings from your handwriting.

9. Size of Script

Do people remark that your writing is so tiny they can't read it? Or
so large that you waste paper because you can get only five or six lines
on an 8½-by-11-inch page? How did you assess the size of your writing? If one of these categories seems to fit, your handwriting is considered out of balance. Not wrong, just out of balance.

Tiny Writing

Persons who write in a tiny script have an easy time with details. In
fact they love nothing better. They delight in focusing on incremen-
tal information, and often end up with careers in research, type design, ancient languages, computer science, or history of just about
anything that interests them, perhaps even law, if it has to do with research. They love anything that will keep them in their heads. Many
inventors, scientists, editors, engineers, and mathematicians tend to
write very, very small.

This spills into their lifestyle. Along with tiny writing is a preference to become invisible and simply disappear at times. If you have
miniscule script you are probably laughing with recognition by now
because it's true, isn't it! Keep laughing—it gets better.

Physically, tiny writers prefer to work, live, and play in small
spaces. Rarely will you find them living in a mansion. If they do,
there will be a safe retreat for them within that mansion, a confined
or closed space where they can spend time alone with their design
work, books, or computers. If they are athletically inclined they usu-

ally select a sport with clearly defined spaces: tennis, volleyball, and racquetball are good examples, or something they can do alone, such as running, bicycling, or swimming.

If your writing is miniscule, by making your writing medium size, your gifts and tastes will not disappear, they will be enhanced and expanded—the difference between living in a closet and occupying the whole house.

If your writing is tiny, that idea probably scares you enough to close this book. Keep reading, for after a few more lines your heart will stop pounding so vigorously. Take a deep breath. Only a few more lines to go. No one is going to make you do anything. You can keep your closet. Now b-r-e-a-t-h-e.

If your script is tiny, you probably prefer small, confined spaces you can call your own; you may thrive on solitude. What will happen as you gradually enlarge your writing is that you will begin to expand your love of miniscule details by stepping out into a larger world in which to share them.

You may begin shaping a career as a public speaker, workshop leader, or teacher. You may even develop a new way of looking at an old science or branch of that science. You may get a patent for that secret invention of yours.

By enlarging your writing you are giving yourself permission to begin the work of expanding your natural talents. You will embrace solitude as a gift rather than compulsively grasping for it.

Large Writing

If your handwriting falls at the opposite end of the spectrum and is extraordinarily large (assuming your eyesight is not failing), by reducing it slightly to medium size, you may notice that details become apparent that previously slipped by unnoticed. You may also find yourself speaking less, listening more, and being more willing to share the spotlight with others.

Persons with extremely large writing do not shy away from center stage. They love nothing better than to be noticed. Often, however, their largeness onstage can show a disregard for the feelings or needs of others.

Persons with very large writing have been known to bulldoze their associates without even realizing it because it is such an ingrained habit. Once it is brought to their attention they can appear quite startled. "Who, me? Why, I wouldn't do that."

If your handwriting falls into one of these extreme categories, you might want to balance it out, for as you bring balance into your handwriting, you bring balance into your life. You can still maintain a huge presence in life, only more sensitively so.

10. Connectivity of Letters Within Words

All Letters Connected

How did you score here? Did you faithfully connect each letter within each word? Or did some of the letters refuse to connect? If you are still living under the shadow of your second-grade teacher's influence, you may have slowed down so you could connect each letter and do it right.

Whoops. Remember now—there is no right or wrong in handwriting. If all the letters are connected, that's fine. If some of them are not connected, that's also fine. The degree of connectivity in your writing simply tells what part of your brain you use to access information.

If all your letters are connected it shows that you rely on logic, reason, and well-tried formulas to arrive at conclusions. If they are unconnected now and again it indicates that you combine reason with insight—also called intuition—before you make up your mind.

Because they deal with equations all day long, you would think that most engineers and scientists write by connecting all their letters. Most of them are convinced they do—until I pull out a magnifying glass.

What I have found is that although the letters appear tightly connected, an enlargement shows this not to be the case. The most innovative, leading-edge scientists, engineers, and inventors I have met write the beginning of a word, pick up their pens from the paper, and rather than leaving a space between the letters, in a nanosecond they place their pens exactly where they were before they picked them up, and finish the word. The funny thing is, they are completely unaware that their pens left the paper. It is a beautiful example of the unconscious mind at work. Their writing ends up looking as though the pen never left the paper because each and every letter appears connected.

It is astonishing how many persons with this habit are convinced they do not pick up their pens midway through a word. When they look through the magnifying glass to see for themselves they are completely taken aback. Their initial reaction is to grab pen and paper and write a few lines to see for themselves. "Oh no! You're right! I can't believe it!" is a common remark as the pen moves across the paper.

This particular writing habit indicates a quick thinker who is extremely intuitive and insightful and would prefer that others not know that he is.

Consistent Connectedness

By connecting each letter as you were taught in penmanship class you allow no room for creativity, insights, or fresh thinking. Consistent connectivity stifles the imagination and the spirit. When each letter is unfailingly attached to the next one, you are locked into living life by someone else's standards, often those of a church, a cultural tradition, family heritage, or even a school system.

You are convinced that life must be lived as it has been set down, without spontaneity or originality. Your relationships can easily flatline into habits rather than being ignited with loving expressions of joy and excitement. Life doesn't change much from day to day. It's not wrong, certainly, but neither is it life-giving.

Unconnected Letters

To balance reason with insight, make it a point to break up any word of five letters or more. When you pick up the pen to do this, leave a visible space between the letters. This is an important point to remember, as that small space represents the gap in which spontaneity lives. It breeds originality and gives permission for unexpressed ideas to burst forth.

This style of writing is called print-script, since it is not completely printing nor is it traditionally connected writing. Write a few lines. See how it feels. Play with it.

If you have consistently connected all your letters most of your life, this may be a radically uncomfortable change to make. If you muster the courage to begin practicing it, you may find yourself holding your breath or breathing very shallowly as you write.

I suggest that before you begin your practice writing sessions you straighten your spine as though you were touching your shoulder blades together, then take a few deliberate deep breaths. As you write, consciously remember to breathe. Keep that back straight; it expands your lungs. Remember—writing habits are not all that you are changing. Once you master this writing change the breathing will take care of itself.

11. Pen Pressure

I asked you to use a ballpoint pen for several reasons, the main one being that the ballpoint pen registers pen pressure more accurately than any other writing instrument.

The surface on which you write is also a factor. If you write on a soft surface, such as a table covered with a cloth, the pen pressure will not register accurately, as the pen will naturally press more deeply into the paper.

Given that you wrote with a ballpoint pen on a firm surface, how did you gauge your pen pressure? Can you feel an impression on the back of the page?

If your fingers pick up slight indentations, you would classify your pressure as heavy. If the writing is reasonably even and clear with little or no pressure through the back of the page, your writing is considered medium. If you write so faintly that it looks as though the pen were whispering, your pressure is considered light.

Heavy Pressure

Pressure on the pen indicates many things, but it basically indicates to what extent you are mentally, emotionally, and physically invested in life. If your focus is laser-like, your personality is intense, and you invest real passion in what you do, your pressure is going to lean toward the heavy side. You do nothing halfway; for you it's all or nothing at all. Even if this intensity is not expressed outwardly, it lives in your spirit.

If you exert heavy pressure on the pen, your senses are alive and fully engaged in your day-to-day activities. You most likely love good food, rich colors, and passionate relationships. You are more sensitive to sounds and aromas than the average person; you may even sense smells when no one else does.

You may tend to run or stride rather than walk. Tiptoeing would not come naturally to you. If you could get your body to slow down long enough, you would be drawn to stop to smell those roses as you race by your neighbor's garden.

As a heavy-pressure writer you wouldn't think of buying a new coat or jacket without first feeling the texture of the fabric. Taste, touch, smell, sight, sound, physical energy, and passion—they are the fuel for the motor that runs your life. If you gauged your pressure as heavy you have probably been called "intense" more than once in your life.

Medium Pressure

If you exert medium pressure on the pen you can still be totally invested in life, but with a more moderate expression of energy. You may feel as deeply as the heavy-pressure writer, but these feelings do not consume you. Like the pressure, they are moderate and express themselves with less passion and intensity.

Light Pressure

If your pressure is faint on the page and I were to ask you to write a few lines pressing harder on the pen, you might rebel at my request. Exerting more pressure on the pen might feel to you like soloing at Carnegie Hall when you have sung only in the shower. You may give it a few halfhearted tries, but would probably end up responding, "I can't. I just can't do it."

Although as a light-pressure writer you may be just as physically present as the heavy- and medium-pressure writers, you do not have the degree of mental or emotional investment in life that they do.

You may be attracted to a quieter, more spirit-centered life; you may find it difficult to be committed for any length of time to projects or relationships; you tend to withdraw from confrontation rather than greet it face-to-face. You may even speak softly.

The degree of pressure on the pen is again only one factor in handwriting. Remember that jigsaw puzzle? One piece of the puzzle is only one piece of the puzzle. Each piece is essential in making the picture complete, and light pressure is only one piece.

12. Writing Implement

What was your answer here? If an assortment of pens and pencils were laid out in front of you, which would you naturally choose? A fountain pen? A felt-tip pen? A ballpoint with a particular width of point? A pencil? This may seem like a trivial question, but the implement of choice is a valuable clue in exploring our attitudes.

Fountain Pen

Do you prefer to write with a fountain pen? If so, you are most likely a lover of the written word and literature, and you delight in things classical. Beauty, depth, and tradition are important to you. People who choose other writing implements may share your interests, but not quite in the same way you do.

Sad to say, a fountain pen is rarely used these days. Like the warm, rich tradition of hand-writing letters, it is fading away. In 1993 the U.S. Postal Service released the statistic that only 4 percent of mail is handwritten.

After all, in these times of instant everything, the fountain pen is at best a nuisance. It is not disposable, needs filling regularly, and on top of that, it may require a blotter and a bottle of ink as a constant companion. Yet there are some of us who relish those inkwells, those blotters, those magnificent writing instruments. Can you tell I am one of them?

Felt-tip Pen

Did you write felt tip as your favorite pen? This type of pen customarily draws a rather thick stroke, and fills in most of the loops and circles as it moves. Quite often the upper and lower zones have no loops at all, but appear as straight sticks instead. There are no accidents in life or in writing. We'll discuss loops in a few pages.

My experience with felt-tip-pen writers is that their lives are based on creating a strong outer image, and they fear being "found out." This does not imply that they are criminal or have committed some nefarious act. It simply says that their outer image is not aligned with who they see themselves to be on a deep inner level. The felt-tip pen allows them to conceal personally held attitudes while presenting another face to the world.

The thick steady line does not indicate heavy or light pressure, does not allow for distinct letter formations, and makes it difficult to draw all but a few loops. It allows the writer to wear the costume of an amorphous personality. For some, it can also be an expression of thumbing their noses at the rest of the world.

If you are an inveterate felt-tip-pen user and want to see if the shoe fits, do this: Go to a store that has a large assortment of pens. Go to the ballpoint pen section and try out a few. See how it makes you feel to write with one.

Remember Noble Truth Number Four: The degree of difficulty in the mastery of a stroke change is directly proportional to the value it will have in your life; the greater the difficulty, the greater the value. If you're willing to expose your talents and gifts, and be more accepting of who you are, accept the challenge of a lifetime: Buy several ballpoint pens in different colors and begin using them exclusively.

For the next forty days put away all your felt-tip pens and write with only ballpoint pens—no other pens, no pencils. In the beginning the change may cause restlessness, anxiety, fear of exposure, or resentment, but keep at it. What you are doing by using a different kind of pen is flinging aside parts of your costume one piece at a time, allowing others to see who you really are. You are leaping from behind the curtain and becoming authentically yourself.

Close your eyes and imagine the positive impact this could have not only within yourself, but in all your relationships. Feel good? You might want to give it a whirl.

Ballpoint Pen

Because of the way it is structured, a ballpoint pen reveals more information about you than any other writing implement. A felt-tip pen conceals pressure; if you press too hard the tip will fray. By pressing on a fountain pen with great intensity, the nib will splay and the ink will splatter—a messy combination.

A Rollerball registers a steady, even line without giving an inkling of pressure on the page. Like a felt tip, it also does not indicate which strokes were emphasized by pressing on the pen and which were diminished by lightening up on it. A Rollerball is a step up from a purely felt-tip pen, however, as it can create clear loops and circles.

Unless you take on a writing practice that requires otherwise, I am not suggesting that you stop using a Rollerball or fountain pen for everyday writing. Nor am I suggesting you use a ballpoint pen all the time—except for the forty-day challenge. I am merely explaining how they reflect the personality. I would suggest, however, that the felt-tip pen and the pencil are the two writing implements to avoid using consistently.

The Pencil

Most of us use pencils at one time or another. I can't imagine carrying down the balance in my checkbook, reconciling my bank statement, or doing a crossword puzzle without one. I often make mistakes that need correcting, and pens are so final.

When I speak of pencil users I am referring to persons who prefer a pencil as their writing implement of choice at least 60 percent of the time.

Did you write down pencil as your preference? If you did, it must have been an uncomfortable stretch for you to fill your page writing in ballpoint pen in the first place, like being asked to wear a wool coat in 90-degree weather. Your mind must have been shouting, "Take that silly thing off. No one wears a coat in this heat!"

Use any analogy you will, a pencil writer prefers a pencil. Period. If you are a confirmed pencil user, read on and see if any of the following fits.

Dedicated pencil users often find it difficult to commit to any project, relationship, or endeavor for a sustained period of time. They carefully avoid situations in which there is no back door, no way out. They find ways to avoid being on target and available. Chameleon-like, they have a tendency to change directions frequently, often right in the middle of something others may have thought was going forward. You can't pin down a pencil writer. Remember—a pencil can be erased.

The cornerstone of a proactive life is commitment. It is the foundation upon which we make our decisions. If you are a pencil writer, the ground on which you stand tends to keep shifting and you may have great difficulty committing to almost anything. This fear has probably gotten you in some hot water in your relationships in the past; it may even have alienated friends, family, associates, and people you truly love.

Although you may not be able to pinpoint the source of your fear, you can begin to dissolve it slowly by the simple act of writing with a pen. As you consistently choose ink over lead, you may experience flashes of your basic fear, but it will no longer have a grip on you. It will begin to feel like a story, a dim memory, and as you choose pen rather than pencil consistently, your fear will begin to fade and eventually disappear.

As you do your daily writing practice, keep Miracle Notes to record the changes. In this way you can see for yourself the day-to-day evolution of what is changing. I guarantee—this one change can improve your relationships dramatically.

As an experiment, why don't you put your pencil aside and for the next forty days pick up only a ballpoint pen and use it unfailingly. Let someone else balance your checkbook, or put that off until after the forty days have elapsed. Do your crossword puzzles in ink—now that's *real* commitment! See what happens.

To strengthen your resolve you may also take on the promise to keep your word, doing what you say you will do, for these forty days. A combination of rigorous honesty and unwavering commitment to your promise can cause enormous anxiety for a longtime pencil user—I'm not pretending it won't. The results can be dramatically effective, however, because you will be shedding old, unwanted habits and putting on new ones that work for you. Only you can decide whether it's worth the effort.

A long-term benefit is that you will be diminishing your fear each time you use that pen. As you move it across the page you are doing something more than writing—you are taking a firm stand to be a committed participant in your own life, and completely accountable for what that means. Such freedom!

13. Slant Direction

The direction in which your handwriting slants indicates many things. When you looked at yours, what did you measure it to be? Because slant is a major factor in handwriting, let me give you a visual to make sure it is clear.

This is a leftward (back) slant: *back*

This is a vertical slant: *vertical*

This is a rightward (forward) slant: *forward*

Yours may not fall into any of these exact categories, as each of these samples is an extreme. I used them so you could be very clear when I refer to a particular slant.

Think of the slant in handwriting as your posture as you go through life. When you are leaning backward you can't run very fast. When you are standing straight you get a 360-degree view. If you lean too far forward you can fall flat on your face. Use this description as a guideline only, for when you consider other patterns in the individual writing, the conclusion can vary.

Leftward or Back Slant

Let me begin by clearing up a myth. We are trained in school—or somewhere else along the line—to assume that anyone who writes with a pronounced back slant is left-handed. Wrong. It simply is not so.

I have seen the handwriting of many thousands of right-handed persons who have a pronounced back slant. I have seen the handwriting of many thousands of left-handers with a decided rightward slant.

Sad but true, many left-handers were taught to arch their arms and hands around the top of the page, holding their pens, so they could write from left to right. By changing the slant of the paper and placing it in the opposite direction ⬦, left-handers can easily avoid that gymnastic feat.

A leftward slant is any slant that causes the handwriting to appear as though it were leaning over backward. It can be slight, it can be moderate, it can be extreme, as in the sample on the previous page. The writer with a consistent leftward slant is someone who is holding back, for whatever reason, from expressing herself authentically in the world.

Back-slanted writers can have an outgoing personality, they can be withdrawn and quiet, or they can respond without going to either extreme. What this slant indicates is someone who is not able to be straightforward about who she really is and what she wants from life. They may be aware of it on a deep inner level, but they slather it over with layers of fear and resignation. They are not being overtly dishonest; they are withholding.

Years ago I met a litigation attorney who was a tiger in the courtroom. Her expertise was family law. She was dedicated to seeing that children who found themselves in the middle of nasty divorce settlements were protected from being placed in abusive settings; she defended the children like a mamma bear would defend her cubs.

After a particularly stress-filled court case she wrote me a note. I had not seen her handwriting before. When I looked at the return address on the envelope my first thought was, "I wonder who lives in Brigette's house." I opened the envelope and pulled out the handwritten note. It was from Brigette. I was shocked. The slant was tilted so far to the left I actually wanted to reach down and straighten it before it flopped over backward. I have seen very few handwriting samples as extreme as hers. Because of her outgoing personality and skill and dedication in the courtroom, at first glance I was puzzled.

As I began to study all of her writing patterns I saw what was going on. She loved children—loved them. More than that I saw that she had a deep commitment to them. Along with her brilliant, professional, and articulate personality her handwriting also showed her to have a broad streak of playfulness, mischief, and innocence. Deep inside she was an outrageously creative child; I saw too that she was a born teacher.

We had lunch a few weeks later. Midway through our meal I asked her point-blank, "Brigette, why are you an attorney?" She put down her fork and looked up, startled. "What do you mean?" she said, looking straight at me with the beginnings of a playful smile. "Do you think I'm not good at what I do?"

"On the contrary—you are excellent at what you do. If I were an attorney I would want to have your same zeal, commitment, and set of ethics. But when I study your handwriting patterns I see that you would much rather be teaching children than rescuing them. So— back to my original question: Why are you an attorney?"

With a wry laugh she responded, "Look, Vimala. My father is an attorney. My mother is an attorney. Two of my brothers are attorneys. My sister is in law school. My brother-the-black-sheep is a doctor. I had no options." Her response made us both laugh at the objective absurdity of it. Her final words, "And no—don't tell me to change my handwriting!" closed that part of our conversation.

Two years later a tragedy struck Brigette's family, and everything she held dear fell apart. As the grief settled, she realized that this was *her* life, and she alone was accountable for how she lived it. To shorten a long story: She went back to school, obtained her elementary teaching credential and is now winning Teacher of the Year awards right and left from the parents of the kindergarten children she teaches. As her attitudes changed, her handwriting changed automatically. It is now vertical, expanded, and clear, and her autograph makes a clear statement of who she is, from the inside out.

Vertical Slant

Handwriting that seems to go straight up and down with little forward or backward movement is considered vertical. Is yours?

If your writing slants vertically about 75 percent of the time you tend to think before you act, ponder a bit before jumping on to someone else's bandwagon, and keep your own counsel. Printscripters with a vertical slant are often engineers, graphic designers, writers, or in some field where clear, creative thinking is a requisite. They are good at putting pieces together.

It is important with slant especially to keep in mind that this is only a small puzzle piece. In order to see what the complete picture looks like, each piece must be connected to the next.

Rightward or Forward Slant

When you came to this question, if you looked at your writing and laughed because there was no doubt whatsoever that your writing slanted forward, you have a pronounced forward slant. If you had to study your writing closely to figure out if it really did lean to the right most of the time, your rightward slant is a moderate forward slant. If it came in somewhere between vertical and almost forward, your rightward slant is slight.

The degree of forward slant is directly related to your responsiveness or reactivity to life's situations. If your slant leans far to the right—*far* to the right—your tendency is to react rather than to respond. You may be so busy reacting to people and situations that valuable nuances often slip by unnoticed—nuances that may have been crucial in making sound decisions. Extremes in handwriting have the same effect as extremes in life. They prevent clear vision.

As a far-rightward-slant writer you may be cause-oriented, energetically supporting groups you believe in. You tend to evaluate people—and sometimes causes—from surface values without much inquiry. In your exuberance you are often blindsided by others or taken advantage of on a regular basis. It's those nuances, those subtle energies you didn't pay attention to as you mentally raced by, that would have alerted you to what was going on. You were so busy reacting, you didn't notice.

If any of this is familiar to you, you might want to concentrate on straightening up your slant a bit. Not so it is vertical, but slightly to the right of that. Just slightly.

Moderate Right Slant

If your forward slant leans to the right but is a little less rightward than the extreme slant we just discussed, you may also react, but perhaps not so instantly or intensely as the writer above.

Slight Right Slant

If your forward slant is ever so slightly right of vertical, I would suggest that you leave it that way. This could be called the ideal slant. *This particular slant* identifies the balanced writer, the one whose tendency is neither to withhold nor explode, but to remain pretty much in center most of the time.

Again, remember that slant is only one part of your handwriting.

The rest of your personality will emerge as you consider pen pressure, margins, and thousands of other small pieces. All the parts must be taken into consideration.

14. Zonal Balance

There are three zones in handwriting: the upper zone, the midzone, and the lower zone. Looking at this diagram will give you a clearer idea of what they represent.

A part of us lives in each zone. The upper zone contains our thoughts, beliefs, knowledge, philosophy, and creative ideas—it is the mental area. The midzone represents everyday life—our bottom line, so to speak.

Think of the two middle lines as railroad tracks. Within this area—the midzone—we carry on our daily life: tying our shoelaces, driving the car, brushing our hair, performing mundane activities.

The lower zone represents our attitude toward relationships and our own sexuality. More than that, it reflects our need for movement and change, and the degree to which we are project-oriented. It also tells whether we prefer many friends, a few, or solitude.

It is obvious that zones are quite an important part of our handwriting and what they represent is quite an important part of our lives. Let's begin at the top.

Upper Zone

Thoughts, beliefs, ideas, creativity, and philosophy all live in the upper zone. Anything that transfers itself into thought form has a home here. The more you live there, the taller or fuller it will be.

Tall Upper Zone

If you tend to live in your head a great deal or love to learn, or would rather *think* about relationships than *be* in them, your upper zone will be rather tall. An exceedingly tall upper zone—three times or more the height of the midzone—indicates a person who has cut himself off from people as a result of his knowledge, imagination, or profession. It's a lonely place to be. A balanced upper zone is about 2 to 2½ times the height of the midzone.

Moderate Upper Zone

If your upper zone is only slightly taller than your midzone it does not mean that you are not intelligent, nor does it mean that you do not think a great deal. It means that your attention is focused more on midzone than upper-zone activities.

Disappearing Upper Zone

If your upper zone is almost missing and upstrokes seem to shrink right into the midzone, barely peeking above it, and your lower zone does the same thing, all of your attention is midzone focused.

A perfect illustration of midzone-focused writing is that of teenage girls. Quite often their script is roundish, all in the midzone, rarely reaching either into the upper zone or dipping down into the lower zone. Writing like this indicates complete absorption in midzone activities. The questions this kind of writer might be asking are, "Did I say the right thing?" "Does he really like me?" "Do I really look good in this color?" all of which are focused in the here-and-now consciousness of the midzone thinker.

For teenagers it's quite normal; they are in the pubescent stage of self-discovery. If your writing looks like this and you are out of your teens, you might begin to have your writing stretch up a little or dip down a little, nudging yourself into other zones to get a feel for what it might activate inside you. As you extend your zones you are beginning to explore what they represent.

Lower Zone

The lower zone is filled to overflowing with information because it indicates where we go into action—or choose not to. It shows how we follow through on our upper-zone and midzone energy. It is the area of activity, project orientation, relationships, sexuality. You can't hide anything in your lower zone. The ideal lower zone is about 2 to 2½ times the height of the midzone.

If you have an abundance of great ideas but get stuck when it comes to implementing them, begin to lengthen your lower zone and create generous loops—not extreme, just generous. Something like this:

This particular kind of loop will also help you to be more self-expressed in your sexual life, for it knocks down barriers to being naturally in action with your feelings. A little added pressure on the pen will help here too, for the heavier the pressure the more intense the investment of energy.

15. Loops

In handwriting, loops are containers. What they contain depends on where they occur. Sometimes loops reflect positive, forward-moving attitudes; at other times they reflect attitudes that are constraining.

At the beginning of this chapter I stated the importance of remembering that virtually all strokes in handwriting can have both a positive and a negative connotation. Loops are a prime exemplar of this guiding principle.

Upper Zone Loops

Loops in the upper zone often occur in the following letters: d, h, l, f, T, and the turn-of-the-century k and b. The only letters in which it is desirable to have upper zone loops are h, l, and f.

If you use the outdated lowercase k and b, I encourage you to begin writing them like this: k, b, as they occur in The Vimala Alphabet. It can give you a new way to look at life and remove obstacles you may not even be aware of.

If you notice loops in the stems of your lowercase d's and T's, make it a practice to become aware of them as you write, then gently remove them. I go into more detail about these particular loops in Chapter Four. For now, let's focus on the appearance of loops in the lowercase h, l, and f.

The ideal h, l, and f loops look just like that. Lean, tall, beginning and ending at the baseline. Each of those parameters is important to keep in mind. If the loops ascend more than two and a half times the height of the midzone, they are out of balance. If they show an extreme by being either exaggerated and puffy or the opposite—retraced—they are also out of balance.

Retraced Upper Loops

By retracing these loops h l f you are withholding a precious part of yourself—your ideas, your beliefs, your dreams about how life can be. Remember, that is what lives in the upper zone. An upper loop that breathes lets the energy that resides there flow in and out, unrestricted. When it is compressed, its air supply is being cut off.

Whenever you catch yourself retracing an upper loop, merely go back, write over it, and expand it; it will make a tremendous difference.

Exaggerated Upper Loops

If you consistently write exaggerated loops in the letters $h\,\ell\,f$, fear and anxiety have nudged you into the world of make-believe, and you may find it difficult existing in ordinary day-to-day life. The world in which you prefer to live is one of fantasy and imagination. If you have a gift for writing, you might consider trying your hand at writing gothic novels, science fiction, or adventuresome children's stories. You would be a natural. Narrowing those upper-zone loops a bit will help you bring your ideas into reality.

Midzone Loops

Because of their particular circle formation, the midzone loops we are going to deal with here occur specifically in the letters a, o, d, g, and q, the five principle letters of communication within the alphabet.

As you know, loops are containers. In the letters a, o, d, g, and q they can occur in several places in the midzone. Most frequently they are seen in the inner left of the circle , in the inner right , or both . Sometimes they can join to create a third inner loop . None of these loops is desirable. Nor is the type of loop that completely encircles the letter such as or .

When loops like these appear it indicates hidden information, facts you are intentionally not being open or clear about, something you are consciously concealing. It is crucial to have the ovals in the letters a, o, d, g, and q expanded and uncluttered with nothing at all inside them or encircling them.

Now and again you may find one or more of these configurations in your writing. Don't panic. Simply be aware of them as you write and change them on the spot. Remember Noble Truth Number Two: The frequency with which a writing habit occurs in your writing is the frequency with which the quality it represents occurs in your life.

If you see these inner loops consistently, that's the time to be concerned. By hiding information about yourself or others it is impossible to be forthright. Not only that, by feeling compelled to withhold information you are also making yourself wrong in some regard. This feeling is often accompanied by an element of guilt or shame. This can have adverse effects not only in your relationships, but also on your health.

This is my very favorite inner-loops story. Years ago I received a writing sample in the mail with the request for an analysis. I'll call the writer Marissa. Inner loops were everywhere in the midzone of her writing. Everywhere. As I studied the sample closely I saw that the writer was holding on to secrets from many years back, secrets that she felt she dared not tell at the risk of losing every friend she had ever had. I did the analysis, mailed it off, and within days I received a phone call. It was Marissa.

"How did you know all that you told me?" was her opening question. "It's all in your writing patterns, Marissa; it's all in your writing patterns" was my reply. Her response was abrupt: "No. You must know me from somewhere; you *must*." After a few minutes we ascertained that we had never met. She began to read a few lines from the analysis and stopped. She was crying. "How could you know? *Nobody* knows."

We agreed to meet. She came to my office the next day and shared the following story. Young and innocent, she and Harvey were teenagers when they were married during World War II. A soldier, he left for the war zone only weeks after the nuptials. Often his letters did not reach Marissa for weeks, and she was desperately lonely. As a result, she had a quick one-night stand with a man whose name she couldn't even remember. It happened only once. She told no one.

Harvey returned, they were blessed with children, and lived almost happily ever after. The "almost" was her secret affair and the plaguing question, "What will happen if Harvey ever finds out?"

As she finished telling me her story I made a suggestion. "To relieve yourself of this burden of guilt, why don't you consider doing two things: First, eliminate all the inner loops from your midzone circle letters. This will help you be straightforward. Second, tell Harvey what happened. It was over thirty-five years ago, and besides, you both love each other so much."

"Oh, I couldn't tell him, Vimala. I just couldn't! I'll do the writing practice, but I just can't tell him," she replied. We chatted a bit longer, and she left.

Three weeks later I received a call. It was Marissa. "Vimala. You'll never guess what happened. You'll never guess. I've been doing my writing every day just as you suggested—no more of those inner loops. I mailed you a letter today so you can see. But that's not why I'm calling you." She was obviously excited. "Last night I decided to tell Harvey my secret. You were right. I just couldn't go on hiding it any longer. I don't know if it was the handwriting changes that made me decide, or whether I simply had had enough, but I just couldn't hide my shame any longer.

"I prepared his favorite meal and we had a candlelight dinner. I told him tonight was special because I had something to share with him. As hard as it was, over dinner I told him what had happened and let him know how awful I had felt about it through the years . . . and I asked him to forgive me." She paused.

"Do you know what he did, Vimala? He just sat there without even looking shocked or amazed. Then he smiled. He put his elbows on the table, rested his chin on his hands, then leaned toward me. 'Marissa, honey, I've known that for over thirty years. I didn't want to let *you* know I knew because I felt it might damage our relationship . . . and I love you too much for that.'"

When they stopped by my office the next day to say thank you, they had the look in their eyes of newlyweds.

Lower-zone Loops

Lower-zone loops come in all shapes and sizes, one for every personality. They represent relationships, movement, sexuality, and change. The length of the *downstroke* into the lower zone reflects the writer's endurance—the degree of energy she or he is willing to expend toward developing a project or relationship. The width and size of a lower-zone loop indicates the amount of energy it contains.

The ideal lower-zone loop looks like this: *g, q, y, j, f.* Each of these loops is considered balanced when it is about the same width as the formation in the midzone, and about twice as long.

Lower loops that are compressed (*q y j z*) reflect withheld energy, a repression or denial. They also let us know that the writer is eclectic when it comes to friendships.

When lower loops are oversized (*g y j z*) it can mean one of many things. It can relate to the writer's expression or repression of sexuality, an overdue need for change, or an inherent need for physical movement. This same loop connotes different mindsets. *Especially* with lower loops, it is extremely important to consider the entire handwriting sample before assessing their meaning, keeping in mind that a loop is only one piece of that complex jigsaw puzzle called the human psyche.

Seeing an abundance of large lower loops in a sample of writing, it would be so easy to say "this person has repressed sexual urges," when in truth she simply has been in a job too long, desperately needs to be out of a relationship, or her body is crying out for exercise. The loop will look the same; you need the rest of the writing to get the whole story.

A lower loop that is consistently short or short and retraced is indicative of writers who focus on reaching goals with the least expenditure of energy. They are not into small talk or prolonged discussion; they are into achieving an objective quickly.

If you have lengthy meetings at your place of work and participants grumble at time being wasted, find someone who is reasonably articulate, has the ability to conduct a meeting, and writes with short lower loops. Then hand him a printed agenda for the next meeting, let him know the length you would like the meeting to be, and put him in charge. You may be astonished at the results. An ordinary two-hour meeting can be compressed into under an hour with all agenda items handled.

16. Angles and Curves

Look at your sample of writing. Did you notice more angles than curves? More curves than angles? Or a balanced amount of each?

Angles

Angles represent analysis and perception; they indicate a tendency toward more mental attributes than social. If you deal with ideas all day long or love to find out facts and information, even in your relationships, you will have more angles than curves in your writing.

Angles at the Top of the Midzone

If the angles tend to occur more often at the top of the midzone ($\mathcal{M}$), your mind spends a lot of time driving into the upper zone searching around for answers. Think of that kind of angle as a laser, piercing into the mental realm.

Angles at the Baseline

If you find more angles at the baseline than at the top of the midzone ($\mathcal{N}$), you love to take ideas apart, analyze them, and put them together in an entirely new form before you are done with them. Your tendency would be to invent, discover, be a trailblazer—if the rest of your handwriting patterns support that trait.

Angles at Both the Top of the Midzone and at the Baseline

If you have angles both at the top of the midzone and at the baseline, you are not only compelled to find answers but to analyze those you receive. Many writers with these characteristics are in a field in which sound and energy are key factors—sound engineers and inventors, for example.

The sound engineers I have worked with hear beyond what ordinary folks hear, and can interpret sounds in a way that appears baffling to those of us who do not have that refined sense of listening. They live in a space between mind and spirit, and can find it a puzzling task at best to be grounded in what some of us call everyday life.

Nikola Tesla is a shining example of an inventor with crisp, clear, analytical thinking. He created an object in his head first, then mentally went through it piece by piece, constructed it, and put it in motion. When his brilliant mind perceived a glitch in its functioning, he corrected it mentally, so that once the device took physical form it ran flawlessly the first time. Here is a sample of his handwriting: tiny and predominantly angled, with just enough curves to indicate his gentle nature.

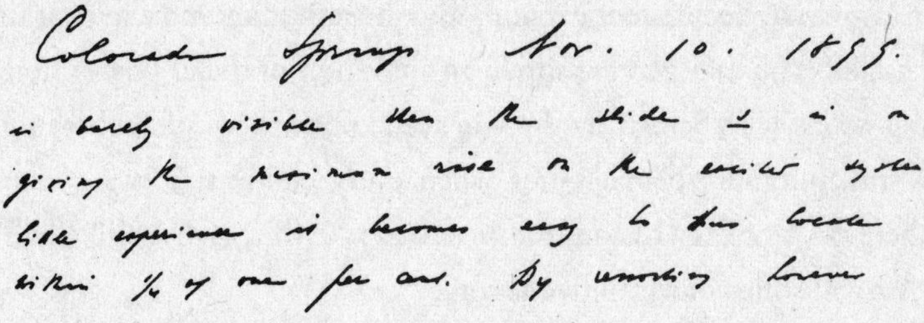

[handwritten sample]

Because this combination of angles indicates inquiry and analysis, writers in other professions can also have them: financial planners, engineers, statistical analysts, and anyone else with mental acumen and the ability to analyze data.

Curves

In handwriting there are two kinds of curves: *garlands,* so called because they look like them (‿) and *arcades* (⋀), again, because they look like them.

Curves, like their shape, are friendly and soft. If you have more curves than angles in your writing you are most likely more social than you are in your head, especially if those curves appear as garlands at the baseline—between letters and at the beginning and endings of words.

Garlands

Garlands occur most frequently at the baseline as connectives linking one letter to the next. They can also occur in letter shapes such as the *U u* or *W w.*

To understand the meaning of a garland, think of a group of persons standing in a circle. The garland is the shape that occurs when each person reaches out her hand to another. Garlands are socially oriented, they are friendly. They say, "Come play with me."

If you have consistent garlands as connectives and no angles at the baseline, you may want to slip in an angle here or there. There's nothing wrong with being friendly—heaven knows the world needs more warm, outgoing people—but when every connective is a garland there is a tendency to connect most letters within each word, a habit that will stifle your intuitive nature.

If you see this tendency in your writing, make it a point to leave spaces between your letters now and again and to slip in angles at the baseline whenever you think about it.

This simple change will allow you to know when it is appropriate to reach out and when it is best to keep your hands to yourself. The angle, the $\vee$ shape, represents discrimination—the ability to choose wisely.

Arcades

An arcade is a common stroke in writing. Did you find any in your writing sample? Again, remember we are seeking balance. A few gentle arcades—lovely. Lots of arcades or retraced arcades—imbalance.

Arcades most naturally occur in the letters *m*, *n*, and *h*. They represent a kind of paternal guardedness, either gentle or compulsive. To know which is represented, the rest of the writing patterns must be studied.

Arcades that are retraced in the midzone (*m* *n* *h*) can reflect extreme traditional thinking and the need to process information in a methodical, step-by-step manner. If this is negative and compulsive it can reflect a mind that is closed to further inquiry, sealed with the comment, "But we've always done it that way." From a positive view-

point it could occur in the writing of someone whose profession de-
mands exactitude, such as a plastic surgeon.

If your arcades seem glued to one another as in the previous example, rather than graceful and free—*m, n, h*—you might want
to pull them apart slightly and let them breathe. These three letters
live in the alphabetical family of Honoring and Expressing, i.e., honoring your gifts and expressing them freely. Above all, let them in-
hale, let them exhale, let them breathe, give them life.

17. Printing Versus Writing

This section is especially devoted to printers. If you print consistently please read it, re-read it and re-re-read it, for it can open you
gently from the inside out and might even cause an explosion of your
well-protected gifts.

In working with people's handwriting I have found that printers
are often talented, gifted, sensitive persons, who, for one reason or
another, do not openly acknowledge their talents. They have stuffed
their real feelings down for so long they may be out of touch with
them; often they cannot even identify the fear that caused them to
begin stuffing their feelings in the first place.

The Litany of Printers usually begins, "I print because no one can
read my writing." Whenever I hear this phrase, my ears perk up. I
have learned to become suspicious of what follows "because."

I invite printers—you, if you print—to entertain the fact that you
print *and* no one can read your writing, not *because.* Unless you have
small-motor-skill problems or a lower than average degree of intelligence, illegibility is not a causative factor in printing.

Printing is a way of protecting yourself. There are countless patterns in writing that do this—illegibility is one—yet none so final
and definitive as printing. There are two kinds of printing: upper-

and lowercase printing and uppercase only, called block printing. Each is significant in its own way.

Upper- and Lowercase Printing

This is the kind of printing we learned in elementary school. Uppercase letters occur at the beginning of sentences and in other appropriate places; there are also lowercase letters. It would be very much like the lines you are reading. This is called upper- and lowercase printing. For short, let's call it u&lc printing.

Printing is a shield usually put in place by a sensitive soul who has been betrayed in one way or another and isn't about to let that happen again. Printing keeps people at a distance by creating a distinct boundary. The u&lc printer has erected a wire fence around himself—more specifically around his feelings and around his heart. The wire fence allows people to come just so close, and no closer. In getting to know a u&lc printer it quickly becomes obvious that a barrier is up.

If you want to tap into your creativity in a big way, and your printing falls into this category, begin now and again to connect a letter or two within your words. Take this on slowly, not compulsively, and see how the change impacts your daily interactions. Play with it. Stand back and see what happens. Keep Miracle Notes.

Block Printers

A person who writes with all capital letters is called a block printer. Because the first reaction of a block printer is to become defensive, if you fall into this category, please, please read on. The next few paragraphs could alter the shape of your future in a positive, exciting, and dramatic way. Remember, I don't know you, so don't take this personally.

You won't find the u&lc printer's fence here. You will find a wall, thick and impenetrable. Behind it are hurts so deep, betrayals so long-standing, and such a terrified need for protection that the wall is fortress-like. After all, blocks are for building walls. As long as the block printing continues, you will never get to know who this person is.

What is behind that wall is often a creative, artistic spirit who has never authentically and fully expressed his gifts to the world. I say "his" since about 90 percent of block printers I have encountered are male.

Another defense mechanism block printers use is a crusty, ego-centered exterior. They can be blustery, loud, arrogant, impatient, even downright rude. It's all part of the wall, the mortar that holds the blocks together, a part of their protection. It's not who they are deep down; it's a defense against having anyone find out the sadness hiding behind their wall.

Police officers and firefighters are often block printers. They tell me that on the forms they fill out at work, they are instructed to block print only; nothing else is acceptable. Fine. But a memo or letter, or notes in a meeting do not constitute a form. Many civil servants use block printing on forms and handwrite their other correspondence.

One of the reasons many firefighters and police officers block print in their regular correspondence is that they have been provided no safe environment in which to express how their experiences have affected them. They assume the outer attitude of "It's all in a day's work," but block printing says their feelings are all walled up inside.

Until I got to know a few of them, I pictured firefighters as people in yellow slickers pointing water hoses at burning buildings. Don't you believe it. They see just as many horrors as police officers do, perhaps even more: Tiny tots accidentally run over by trucks, children dying of asphyxiation or third-degree burns, women and children beaten bloody and senseless by a raging drunk husband and father. It's no wonder so many of them block print.

Other block printers have had events occur in their lives that have caused them to close off from intimacy or from trusting their feelings with another. One example might be a thirteen-year-old boy who has a crush on a girl and tells his best friend with the admonition that he not tell anyone. His friend decides to have fun, and tells everyone he can think of. Boy number one feels deeply betrayed, and not long after he begins to block print. There are as many stories as there are block printers.

To begin dismantling your wall in a safe, healthy manner, I suggest that you as a block printer gradually begin to use upper- and lower-case printing. It will gently and safely begin to remove the blocks and allow you to peek around the wall to see if it's safe. You will still be protected, for you will slowly be replacing the wall with a fence, which, although it is protection, is a little less daunting to others.

Once you've printed in this way for about forty days, begin to connect a few letters now and again—not all of them, just a few, now and again. As I told the u&lc printer, play with it and notice how much freer you feel inside.

Remove the protection gradually—no need for dynamite here. Slowly, gently, begin to print-script. By doing this consistently you will also be releasing your need to be defensive. The most liberating part of all is that you are giving yourself the opportunity to refresh, revitalize, and express those talents you have concealed for so long. Not only that, your authentic self can finally be out in the open, walls down.

A well-known high-profile executive, a client of mine, had been a longtime block printer; as he began the transition from all uppercase to upper- and lowercase writing, then into print-script, he laughingly said he actually felt giddy as a new sense of freedom to be himself emerged.

18. The *th* Ligature

How many of these did you find in your writing sample? This little stroke is important in developing and maintaining flexible relationships of all kinds: personal, business, financial, spiritual, you name it. It represents a fluid, quick thinker, one who can flow from one concept to the next while remaining open and inquisitive.

If you have an abundance of *th* ligatures in your writing, keep them. They are yours; you have earned them. You may also find a ligature creeping in, however, wherever the *t* leads into another letter such as the *to*, *ti*, or *te*. Although it still represents a free-flowing mind, it does not have the overwhelmingly positive connotation of the *th* ligature.

Why? Because the crossbar is flowing into a midzone letter and in order to flow forward it needs to stay low on the stem. This is something you do not want to do, as the *t* crossbar needs to be on the top of the stem. When we discuss the letter *t* in more detail, you will see why.

The *th* ligature you want to avoid looks like this: *th*. It is called a bowl-stroke ligature. Since the *t* crossbar indicates willpower, and this one has a distinct curve in it, it is saying, "I know I'm bright, I know I'm talented, but I don't know where I'm going." Retain the ligature but change the crossbar into a straight, upward-directed one that has purpose and drive. In no time at all you will begin to have a sense of direction.

19. Your Autograph

Well! Who are you? Better yet, how do you want the world to see you? Your autograph is a major clue to the identity you wish to convey in the world. Is it large or small? Is it illegible or is it easy to read? Do you encircle it or draw through it? Is one name easy to read and the other rather thready or indistinct? Is it underscored? By looking at your writing, can you tell the autograph was written by the same person?

Persons who are sure of themselves, self-reliant, open to life, open to others, and open to their unique expression of life have an autograph that is distinct, legible, and exuberant. At a glance it is easy to tell that the autograph and handwriting were written by the same person.

Compare your handwriting sample with your autograph. Is all of this true of yours? If not, and you'd like to balance it out, here are a few things to consider.

Make sure the uppercase letters are 2 to 2½ times the height of the lowercase, no more, no less. As for size, if you tend to shrink back from personal interactions and want to keep it that way, keep your autograph small. If you would rather be more social and outgoing, have it a bit on the large side.

If you want to be at ease relating in a more interactive way, able to socialize as well as enjoy solitude, speak as well as listen, dance as well as pray, then you want to avoid any extremes in your writing, especially in your autograph.

Make sure the midzone is gently expanded. By that I mean neither compressed—*Now is the*—nor exaggerated—*now is.*

The midzone is the area of everyday living, the area of the humdrum activities of day-to-day life. By keeping it reasonably expanded you are letting yourself be open and expressed; you are giving yourself the space to breathe and naturally be who you are and allowing others to do the same.

Again, have your zones in balance. By doing so, all areas of your life—spiritual, mental, emotional, and physical—will be healthy, alive, and ready for action. Your relationships will take on more substance and you may find that both work and play are filled with a sense of appreciation and gratitude.

Encircling your name or initial is the same as putting yourself in a cocoon. Drawing a line through your name is crossing yourself out.

If your first name is clear and your last name is an indistinct squiggle, you base your image on your personal identity. If your last name is easy to read and your first name is virtually illegible it means that your heritage is more important to you than who you are as an individual.

In designing your autograph create healthy letter formations with no exaggerations, fussy curlicues, or embellishments. The ideal is to be simple, flowing, and eloquent.

Underscore

An underscore is a lovely finishing touch—not just for appearances, but as a statement of your ability to be self-reliant and comfortable with notoriety. Have it curved, gentle, and extending from the beginning of your first name to the end of your last name.

The underscore represents a platform on which to stand. Make it gentle and flowing, yet stable. You can draw it in one of two ways. The first way is to finish writing your name, pick up the pen and draw it from left to right.

A second way is possible if your last name ends with a letter that lends itself to creating a *paraph* that will naturally go in a leftward direction. Remember to have the final stroke going off in a rightward direction.

Susan Adams

Design an underscore that reflects your spirit! Because I am inordinately fond of eagles, I swirl mine to resemble an eagle's wings, like this:

20. The Overview

With these nineteen points to consider, look at your handwriting one point at a time and list the changes you might want to make. Since unlined paper and the landscape direction are givens, go down the list beginning with number three, Outer Margins, and number these potential changes in order of priority, number one being the most important change you want to make. Once you have done this, set your list aside as you read Part Two.

Part Two

THE ALPHABET

Chapter 4
THE FAMILIES OF THE ALPHABET

Just as each stroke, angle, garland, margin, and space we create on the page outlines the plot, the letters of the alphabet fill in the details and tell the story. Each letter is a personalized statement of the attitudes that continue to shape our self-image, just as the rest of our handwriting patterns are general assessments. Each letter is not randomly shaped, but formed in a specific way that has evolved through time.

Each letter of the alphabet has a rich and fascinating heritage. Like any family tree, some letters have been around for centuries, others are comparatively new. Because this book is not intended as an historical study but rather as a guide to personal growth, it is with this in mind that we begin a brief overview of the letters.

Because of my deep kinship with them, now and again I will slip in facts about the letters to increase their aliveness for you. Not to do so would be like introducing you to faces and names with no background.

I am going to provide you with an inside look at the interactive family dynamics within the alphabet and extend an invitation to use what you learn as a means of becoming more self-aware, and accelerating your own personal growth.

Rather than opening the family album only for show, I will describe ways to make the healthiest letter formation possible, the one that will help you achieve a balance of its particular quality and, if consistently written, to maintain it in your life.

Like any living organism, each letter contains a unique and powerful energy. Although there is no right or wrong way to make a letter, there is a way to shape letters that allows you to reconnect with a deep place within and to express that unique relationship outwardly.

The letters as I present them are not in the familiar A-B-C-D order. Within the alphabetical family are seven smaller families, and it is within the framework of that relationship that I introduce them. The order in which they occur reflects our human pattern of growth and awakening, our emergence from infancy through maturity into wisdom.

Family of Communication: *A a, O o, D d, G g, Q q, P p*

Family of Learning & Evaluating: *Y y, U u, W w, V v*

Family of Honoring & Expressing: *M m, N n, H h*

Family of Insight: *L l, E e, I i, J j*

Family of Applied Creativity: *F f, R r, S s*

Family of Status: *T T, K k, B b*

Family of Trusting & Inner Authority: *C c, X x*

Contentment: The Letter Zed (*Z Z z*) stands alone.

Chapter 5
THE FAMILY OF COMMUNICATION

Aa, Oo, Ðdd, Ggg, Qq, Pp

Aa: The Letter of Stardom

As far back as written history goes, the letter *A a* is the first letter of almost all phonetic alphabets. In our Roman alphabet it represents our initial entrance into the world as a soul carefully wrapped in the disguise of an ego or personality.

In handwriting, the letter *A a* reflects how we express that ego in daily life and the degree of sensitivity or comfort we have about our physical self-image. If the writer is going bald and is self-conscious about it his *A a* will look one way; if he accepts his approaching baldness with alacrity, it will look another. Being overweight, having an unusual nose or ears, curly or straight hair—the writer's attitude toward any personal physical attribute is reflected in the letter *A a*, for the response is triggered by ego.

The letter *A a* is the head of the Communication Family, for it is from our ego that our self-image is formed and through it that we act, react, and interact.

Uppercase $\mathcal{A}$

This is called the Star $\mathcal{A}$. It reflects a willingness to use our personality to go beyond itself and be center stage without self-interest—to be the Star, ego-free. It is the only uppercase $\mathcal{A}$ you want to make, especially if you are fortunate enough to have one as the initial of your first name.

The one we were taught in penmanship class is called the Easter Egg $\mathcal{A}$, an extension of the lowercase a. Because of its roundness—a manifestation in writing of ego-ness—it keeps us playing the ego game. The Star $\mathcal{A}$ with its initial swooping sense of ascension, its grounded vertical stroke and ending tie loop, gives us the ability to transcend ego and move into spirit. Write a few lines of each and feel the difference for yourself.

Considerations:

1. Begin with a gentle, curved introduction. I call this the Lincoln foot, after Abraham Lincoln, who began his name with this stroke. It brings in the qualities of playfulness and warm humor, and reaffirms the desire to reach out to others in a sincerely altruistic manner.

2. Make the height 2 to 2½ times as tall as the midzone.

3. Create an inverted V shape at the top.

4. Drop straight down to the baseline, creating a right angle.

5. Curve back to the left, crossing over the initial upstroke, creating a loop.

6. Finish the stroke in a rightward direction.

7. Do not pick up the pen from the moment you begin until the letter is complete.

Lowercase *a*

Considerations:

1. Always begin at the top of the midzone.

2. Create an oval that is:
   - uncluttered, with no interference inside the oval;
   - clear, with no muddiness;
   - gently expanded horizontally, neither too lean nor perfectly round, but gently in between;
   - closed top and bottom.

3. As you come down to the baseline, keep the downstroke connected to the oval as far as possible before ending with a gentle garland to the right.

Personal Application of the Letter *A a*

If you find it difficult to be center stage unself-consciously, yet have a driving need to be there, whether it be in business, entertainment, speaking, or in the spotlight in some other way, this elegant letter will give you permission to play that role naturally, not from ego but from that secret place within that wears no costume.

O σ: The Letter of Verbal Communication

Like the letter *A a*, the letter *O σ* is once again the ego, as reflected by the midzone oval. Rather than expressing ego through consciousness of physical mannerisms or appearance, the letter *O σ* reaches out by speaking. It is the letter of verbal communication.

The stroke that often finishes the lowercase *σ* is called a *bridge stroke* because it creates a means of reaching the other side, which the letter *σ* does through speech.

Combined with other factors in the writing, it often connotes a person who is gifted in the ability to work with her hands. It is not unusual to find this stroke in the writing of massage therapists, weavers, bricklayers, and artists of all kinds. By adding the element of tiny writing, it can indicate a person who excels with small, organized details, such as a computer programmer.

The σ can also stand alone in handwriting, with no bridge stroke *O*. Written in this manner it reflects our willingness to be frank and open and to speak courageously, especially when we may be challenged. I am speaking here of handwriting, not printing.

Uppercase *O*

Considerations:

1. In a clockwise direction, beginning and ending at the top, fill both the upper zone and midzone with this letter. Clockwise may be unfamiliar but it is important, as it keeps the energy moving forward. With only a little practice it will feel natural.

2. Draw an oval that it uncluttered, clear, and gently expanded horizontally.

3. Make sure it is closed at the top and the bottom.

Lowercase σ

Considerations:

1. Begin at the top of the midzone.

2. Draw an oval that is uncluttered, clear, and gently expanded horizontally.

3. When made to be freestanding, write the oval in a clockwise direction, beginning and ending at the top.

4. When ending with a bridge stroke, begin in a counterclockwise direction with the final stroke ending at the top of the midzone, to the right.

Personal Application of the Letter O o

The O o gives you the ability to speak openly, clearly, and deliberately. It allows you to be sure of yourself when you communicate and to be disinclined to sugarcoat the truth or to lie. It brings into your speaking the element of clear, gentle firmness rather than a bulldozing or dictatorial energy. It gives you the ability to make your thoughts known clearly. If these qualities are a must in your life, this may be the letter you want to begin practicing.

$Ðdd$: The Letter of Sensitivity

The letter $Ð$ d is a reflection of who I am in the world, just as its cousin the T t reflects what I do. The $Ð$ d indicates the degree of sensitivity we have in regard to how others see us. It is the ego at risk, at the mercy of the opinions of others. As the third member of the Communication Family, it again is the letter a, the ego self, expressing itself uniquely.

The a creates the circular ego shape and returns to the baseline, which represents everyday life. The o either stands alone or reaches out with a bridge stroke as a means of communicating.

The d creates the ego shape, then ascends into the upper zone, the mental area, periscope-like, scanning the environment and asking the question, "What are they saying about me?" The letter $Ð$ d reflects our sensitivity to criticism, our ability or lack of ability to draw boundaries, and the degree of skill and compassion with which we handle the challenge of confrontation.

Uppercase *Đ*

Considerations:

1. Begin with a firm *downstroke* to the baseline.

2. Pick up the pen. Starting at the top of the first stroke, inscribe a rightward arc.

3. End with a gentle forward-reaching loop inside the arc at the baseline. This causes the energy of the letter to flow forward into the rest of the word.

Lowercase *d*

Considerations:

1. Begin at the top of the midzone.

2. Draw a circle that is uncluttered, clear, and gently expanded horizontally.

3. Make sure it is closed top and bottom.

4. Extend the upstroke 2 to 2½ times the height of the midzone.

5. As you come down to the baseline, retrace the upstroke.

6. Make sure it is retraced. Do not allow a loop to form in the stem. A loop in the *d* stem indicates sensitivity to criticism; the larger the loop, the greater the sensitivity.

7. End with a gentle garland at the baseline.

Alternate Formation *d*, the Self-reliant *d*

This letter is encouraged for writers who consistently look to others for answers rather than trusting the adequacy of their own inner resources. It assists the writer in being more straightforward, direct, and self-referred.

Considerations:

1. Beginning in the upper zone, draw a firm downstroke to the baseline.

2. Without picking up the pen, continue by drawing an oval that is uncluttered, clear, and gently expanded.

3. End with a slight underscore to the right.

4. Make sure it is closed at the top and bottom.

5. Do not pick up the pen until the letter is complete.

Personal Application of the Letter *Ð d d*

If your feelings get hurt easily and you find it difficult if not impossible to speak up for yourself or to define personal boundaries without blame, this is the letter you might want to begin practicing.

Well drawn, it can appreciably reduce the strain and stress you may be causing yourself in relationships because of your inability to say what it is you want, or let it be known how you are being affected by another's actions or words.

It allows you to speak from the position of the witness rather than the victim, and thus reduces your inclination to gossip. It gives you the power to speak from your accountability in a relationship or interaction rather than putting it entirely in the other person's lap.

This is a power letter. Can you tell? To experience the transformational effects of this letter, you may want to begin practicing it today.

G g g: The Letter of Prosperity

The letter *G g g*, with its midzone oval, once again reflects the ego. It is the first letter of the Family of Communication to dip into the lower zone, the zone of relationships.

This richly intense letter emerged as an identity separate from the letter *C c* from which it sprang. Above all, when you write it keep it soft and flowing, totally free from angles, remembering that angles reflect mental energy or analysis; curves reflect heart energy.

Just as the letter $C c$ mirrors the imprint our mothers made on our psyches, the letter $G g g$ reflects our attitudes toward male authority figures, echoing back to who our fathers were for us—an impact closely linked to our willingness to welcome or deflect personal acknowledgement, deserved praise, and prosperity.

Persons whose surname begins with the letter G are often wealthy in one area of their lives. Mohandas Karamchand Gandhi, spiritually; George and Ira Gershwin, musically; Francisco Goya, artistically; Bill Gates, financially. If prosperity is missing in any area of your life, this is the letter to wrap your pen around.

Uppercase G

Considerations:

1. Draw a soft three-quarter circle open to the right, filling both the upper- and midzone.

2. Follow this with a soft, non-angular stroke that does not touch the first stroke. This is the only uppercase letter made with two separate strokes in which it is desirable not to have the strokes touching.

Lowercase g

Considerations:

1. Always begin at the top of midzone.

2. Draw an oval that is uncluttered, clear, and gently expanded horizontally.

3. Drop into the lower zone, creating a lower loop that is 2½ times the length of the height of the oval.

4. Create a loop on the left of the downstroke that is the same width as the baseline oval formation.

5. Return to the baseline, barely brushing against the base of the oval as you gently finish the stroke in a rightward direction.

The Lowercase Figure-Eight g

This letter formation is encouraged in the lowercase for anyone who wants to tap into creativity she knows lives somewhere deep inside, a part of her she has not yet been able to access, or to access only intermittently. Merely looking at its shape gives you a clue as to its fluidity and grace.

To experience the magic of this letter at its most outrageous, go outside and with your fingers trace its shape largely in the sand or the earth, or use your arms and hands—left and right alternately—to inscribe it in a generous sweeping motion in the air. Do it several times. Feel it come alive.

To further enhance the evocative nature of this letter, use it with the $\mathcal{E}\ \varepsilon$, for each reflects the writer, the musician, the counselor—the person who *is* her profession and is keenly attuned to that inner voice that prompts her in what to write, play, or say.

It is also an excellent choice for anyone who wants to increase her ability to flow with thoughts and insights and express rather than resist them. If you have a lowercase g somewhere in your name, by all means use the figure-eight g from now on, especially in your autograph.

Because of its openness in the midzone and its completely fluid motion, the figure-eight g not only chisels away at writer's block, it also assists in a softening of interactions with others, the lower zone being the zone of relationships.

Write a few lines of words that contain the lowercase g using the figure-eight g each time; then write the same words using the regular g. See if you don't feel a dramatic difference.

Considerations:

1. Begin the initial stroke as a clean, open c at the top of the midzone. It is important not to have a loop in this c formation.

2. Extend the natural curve into the lower zone, creating a loop that is soft and flowing, about 2½ times the length of the height of the midzone.

3. Finish the loop by crossing the baseline, ending to the right.

Personal Application of the Letter G g g

Do you downplay your accomplishments? Are you constantly being overlooked for promotions? Do you hesitate far too long before asking someone out for a date—decide not to and then regret it? Are you self-conscious when acknowledged and feel awkward accepting sincere compliments or praise for a job well done? If your answer to any of these questions is yes and you'd rather it were no, the letter G g g is the companion you want by your side.

Practice it with rigor until you feel your pen begin to sing. If you make an uppercase G similar to this ᘜ or this ᘜ, practice especially the soft, C-shaped uppercase G.

One of my clients who was a practicing attorney when he first came to see me, but is now a published author, told me that it felt like he was dismantling a dam each time he wrote his new G g. Within a six-week period of consistent writing practice the dam had crumbled and the energy flowed freely; he began to write his book.

Q q : The Letter of Selfless Service

The letter Q q is a magnificent letter, one of my favorites. Again, as a member of the Family of Communication it has the lowercase midzone oval representing the ego. Like the lowercase q, it drops into the lower zone, the zone of relationships.

Unlike the q, however, the q loop is formed on the right side of the downstroke as it ascends to the baseline. This particular loop formation reflects relationships not to particular individuals, as does the left-tending loop, but to one's desire to serve humanity at large. The $Q q$ then reflects burning up the ego—the midzone oval—in service to others.

I fondly call it the Mother Teresa Letter, for it exemplifies her life so clearly. Her comment, "We can do no great things—only small things with great love," is a perfect embodiment of the letter $Q q$.

The only other letter that has a loop off to the right in the lower zone is the letter f, which is also related to reaching out to others. It has a different flavor, however, which we shall explore later.

Uppercase Q

Considerations:

1. In a clockwise direction, beginning and ending at the top, fill both the upper zone and midzone with this letter.

2. Draw an uncluttered, clear, and gently expanded oval.

3. Make sure it is closed at the top and bottom.

4. Draw a soft tail, part in and part out of the circle, at the baseline. A bit of the tail may drop beneath the baseline if you prefer. Remember to keep it liquid and avoid angles.

Lowercase q

Considerations:

1. Begin at the top of the midzone.

2. Draw an oval that is uncluttered, clear, and gently expanded horizontally.

3. Drop into the lower zone, creating a lower loop that is 2½ times the length of the height of the oval.

4. Bring the loop up on the right of the downstroke, creating a loop that is the same width as the oval formation.

5. At the baseline, reach to the left of the initial downstroke and create a *tie stroke* at the base of the oval.

6. Finish with a vigorous stroke to the right.

Personal Application of the Letter Q q

If you have an inner calling to set up soup kitchens, introduce literacy classes, create a program similar to Habitat for Humanity, or create some other outreach facility that you know would be a step toward solving a social problem, begin today to write the letter Q q in a committed manner. Since no word in our English language ends with this power-packed letter, when you practice q as an ending letter, you get to make up your own words.

The effects of this particular letter change are almost always immediate, so be certain to keep your Miracle Notes current. By doing so it will become apparent that your commitment is the energy that fueled the outcome.

P p: The Letter of Self-lovability

The letter P p is a stepchild of the Communication Family, since the midzone circle is not the primary but the secondary stroke, and the midzone formation is a three-quarter circle rather than an oval. Although it is in the same family, the bloodline is just a little different. This most challenging letter reflects our own degree of self-lovability and self-worth, the fundamental attitudes we need to master in the process of maturity, and is directly related to the ego.

Uppercase *P*

Considerations:

1. Beginning at the top of the upper zone, draw a firm downstroke to the baseline.

2. Pick up the pen.

3. Create a full arc to the right, ending with a soft inner loop to the right. Do not let this arc compress; keep it full and expanded.

Lowercase *p*

Considerations:

1. Draw a firm downstroke into the lower zone.

2. Either pick up the pen or retrace back up the downstroke.

3. Create a full arc to the right, ending on the baseline with a soft inner loop to the right. As with the uppercase, do not let this arc compress or become narrow.

Personal Application of the Letter *P p*

If your tendency is to do things to please other people because you want them to like you, or if you tend to get depressed easily, this powerhouse of a letter can help you get in balance, beginning from a place of "I am perfect for the role I am playing in life." When you yourself feel "less than," it becomes a mountainous task to love others. If it's as natural as breathing for you to find fault with just about everyone—including yourself—the letter *P p* may be your guardian angel.

Chapter 6
THE FAMILY OF LEARNING
AND EVALUATING

Yy, Uu, WWww, Vv

Yy: The Letter of Self-acknowledgment

The letter *Y y* has quite a history. It is called the Letter of Pythagoras, for it is traditionally believed that he first designed it to look like this: **Y**, called it *upsilon,* and gave it tremendous significance.

He said the vertical stem represented our life path from birth to adolescence. At the top of the stem we are greeted with a **V** shape. Pythagoras called it a fork in the road, saying that it is at this point we choose to take the narrow road of self-discipline or the broad road of pleasure.

Although the shape has changed slightly, it still represents choices: the decision to pass your unique gifts off as unimportant and continue to dodge them, or to acknowledge and express them openly.

Uppercase *Y*

Considerations:

1. Starting from the top of the upper zone, create a deep, expanded garland with straight sides.

2. Have the right side slightly lower than the left.

3. Drop into the lower zone, creating a generous loop about 2½ times the length of midzone height.

4. Return to the baseline, barely brushing the base of the garland as you finish the stroke in a rightward direction.

Lowercase *y*

Considerations:

1. A miniature of the uppercase *Y*, occupying mid- and lower zones.

2. Give the garland a distinct shape with straight sides.

This letter will have more meaning for you once we look at the lowercase *h*, as the *y* and the *h* are mirror letters. The *y* uses ideas and creativity, remaining open to the upper zone. The *h* uses feeling and gut instinct, being open to the lower zone. More about this when we come to the *h*.

Personal Application of the Letter *Y y*

If you have a half-finished novel hiding in a sock drawer, or a secret invention that will make you millions yet you keep putting off applying for that patent, this is the letter you want to begin practicing religiously. Within no time at all you will find yourself speaking highly of your own work, giving your unique product your own name, and reaching out to support others who are struggling to do the same. It is not a letter of puffed-up pride but one of honest, authentic assessment of the value of your contribution to others.

$\mathcal{U}u$: The Letter of Openmindedness

Just look at this letter. Now that you know ideas live in the upper zone, you can see how the $\mathcal{U}u$ is a natural receptacle for knowledge. When the garland is deep and expanded with straight sides, new ideas fall freely into this empty vessel. In the tradition of the Native American Tiwa tribe the letter $\mathcal{U}u$ lives in the center of the medicine wheel representing the void, the great emptiness, waiting to be filled.*

Uppercase $\mathcal{U}$

Considerations:

1. Starting at the top of the upper zone, create a deep, moderately expanded garland with straight sides.

2. It is important not to let the sides curve inward.

3. End with a gentle garland off to the right at the baseline.

Lowercase u

Considerations:

1. Draw a miniature of the uppercase $\mathcal{U}$, occupying the midzone.

Personal Application of the Letter $\mathcal{U}u$

This letter helps us keep an open mind to new or unfamiliar information; it helps us loosen our mental reins and sincerely invite views that may be contrary to ours. Who would benefit from practicing it? Most of us. It lends particular power to those of us who act as though—and are sometimes convinced that—we have all the answers, we know how it is, and that what anyone else has to say is of little or no value.

*_Being and Vibration_ by Joseph Rael. Oklahoma: Council Oak Books, 1993.

Several years back I had a client whose company was on the verge of bankruptcy. He was desperate to save it yet nothing he did seemed to work—not revised business plans, not hiring and firing, not having endless board meetings. The bank was breathing down his neck, speaking of foreclosure.

The only reason he came to see me was, in his own words, "At this point I'll try anything." "Even changing your handwriting, Doug? This is a commitment to write every day, you know—not just some half-baked maybe-I'll-do-it-and-maybe-I-won't kind of thing" was my response.

"Well, it sounds absolutely absurd to me, but nothing else has worked, so, yes, even changing my handwriting" was his clipped reply. We got to work.

I had him write a full page on unlined paper. When he handed it to me it was instantly apparent that the attitude destroying his company was his own closed-mindedness. He listened to no one. *No* one. Take advice? No way. Hover and control? It was his management style. I suggested he begin altering several key writing patterns, among which was the letter $\mathcal{U}u$, for I felt it would have the quickest and most powerful impact. It did, with a jolt.

He took on his writing practice with fierce determination. After two days he called me. In a shouting/teasing manner he barked, "This isn't easy you know, Vimala. The damn pen wants to do its own thing!" Through my laughter I asked, "Who's moving the pen, Doug, who's moving the pen?!" Then *he* laughed—and picked up his pen and began writing again.

Within a few weeks he decided to have a weekly meeting, the purpose of which was for him to listen—just listen—to what his managers had to say, with the promise that no one would be fired for being honest.

The first week there was a lukewarm, not-quite-trusting response.

Once Doug insisted that his request was on the up-and-up, his managers began to ease their comments and complaints onto the table one at a time, testing the waters. At first Doug was shocked and angry, but as he kept his promise to listen he realized that *he* was the problem. He discovered that although his staff was creative and dedicated, they were shy about offering suggestions for fear of being ignored, put down, or fired. Wake-up call number one.

Each week one of these "listening" meetings was held. In the next few months company attitudes began to shift. As Doug listened—really listened—he realized that although some of his key employees had far less education than he, they knew their part of the job far better than he did. He began to pull way back, stopped micromanaging, and the company began to get on its feet again. Within six months it was operating in the black; within a year it was doing so well the bank granted him an additional loan.

My continuing call during this time was always, "Watch those $\mathcal{U}u$'s, Doug, watch those $\mathcal{U}u$'s!"

If there's a Doug inside you, you might want to take on practicing this great little letter. You may find it not to be as easy as it looks. Is it worthwhile? You decide.

$W\,w\,\mathcal{W}\,w$:
The Letter of the Teacher

Here we have the double-u, or *double vey* as the French would say. The garland on the left is the letter $\mathcal{U}u$, representing a willingness to be open to new information. The garland on the right is again the letter $\mathcal{U}u$. Placed to the right of the first $\mathcal{U}u$, it represents the willingness to teach what we know. The $W\,w\,\mathcal{W}\,w$ is the letter of the teacher.

Persons who are unsure of the worth of what they have to teach, or have difficulty considering themselves as teachers, often close up the right garland of this letter W. If it is not closed, it is impaired in some other way. It can be quite narrow (W) or actually tied off (W). If you know you are here to teach something, even if you're not quite sure what that is, read this section carefully. The letter $W \, w \, W \, w$ has a way of dramatically altering one's awareness.

Uppercase W

Considerations:

   1. Two connected deep garlands, as for the letter U.

Uppercase W

Considerations:

   1. Two deep angles, as for the letter V, touching at the top.

   2. For both the W and W, create a clear division between the two sections.

   3. It is important to keep both U or V shapes open at the top.

Lowercase w

Considerations:

   1. Make garlands with straight sides and a clear division between them, occupying the midzone, ending in a bridge stroke.

Lowercase w

Considerations:

   1. A miniature of the uppercase w, occupying the midzone.

In selecting which $W \, w \, W \, w$ to write, remember what the shapes mean. The function of the garland is to receive information; the function of the angle is to analyze it.

Personal Application of the Letter $Ww\,Ww$

If people you know have urged you to be a teacher, deep down you know you'd be good at it, yet you have a real hesitancy to begin the process involved in setting all that up, this is your letter. No doubt about it. Teaching need not be in front of a classroom. It can be as a motivational speaker, a writer, a minister, or in an allied field. Begin to practice the letter $Ww\,Ww$ then stand back to see what part of you awakens.

Vv: The Letter of Discernment

The letter Vv reflects the indispensable quality of a self-determined life. It is the letter of discernment, choosing wisely from one's own value system. Just as an angle at the baseline represents the ability to analyze information, the pointed Vv represents a discriminating mind.

To create a life that is based on choices you make and values you hold dear, keep your Vv's pointed at the baseline. Make sure they do not loop at the baseline (Y) but are pointed with space between the lines that form the angle. Do not *ever* introduce this fabulous letter with a *detrose loop* ($\mathcal{V}$). This tight and tiny loop contains suspicion, envy, jealousy, and an attitude of egocentrism. It is embedded with fear and severely restricts gratitude and generosity.

Nor do you *ever* want the point to become a garland ($\mathcal{V}$), for in doing so you are saying, "Here. You choose for me. I don't have a mind of my own and I'm afraid to decide without someone else's approval."

Uppercase V

Considerations:

1. Pointed, always.
2. Soft arc off to the right.

Lowercase v

Considerations:

1. A miniature of the uppercase, occupying the midzone.

Personal Application of the Letter Vv

I know this letter intimately and have experienced the life-changing effects it can have. Beginning to practice this letter daily is like shedding an old costume that others have made for you, and donning attire made of fabric and in a style you yourself have handpicked.

If you feel that your life is not your own because you keep following what other people say rather than doing what you really want to, begin practicing the letter Vv right away. It reinforces your ability to make your own decisions. And remember, if things don't turn out exactly as you had planned, you can always change your mind. Choices are not forever, but your life is.

Don't be fooled by the simplicity of two little lines touching at the baseline; this letter is power packed. Try it on. See how it fits. You may be in for the surprise of your life.

Chapter 7
THE FAMILY OF HONORING AND EXPRESSING

M M m, N N n, H h

M M m : The Letter of Divine Grace

The letter *M M m* is the letter of valuing solitude, relating effortlessly in one-on-one relationships, and having the ability to flow with the energy of a group. It reflects being with people and situations just as they are, trusting, expecting nothing of them, and allowing the relationships to flow. I call it the Letter of Divine Grace, for when we give up the need to control, it has permission to function.

There are four parts to an *M M m*, each of which is equal in importance. The first is to introduce this letter gently. Do not ever begin this letter with an angle (*m*). A humor flourish with the arcaded *M* or the playful Lincoln foot with the garlanded *M* are ideal.

The second point to remember is, if you make the arcaded *M m*, make very sure you pull the arcades apart near the baseline rather than tracing back up over them (*m*). This is true with the *m*, the *n*, and the *h*. It is the most crucial factor to keep in mind when forming these letters. *Crucial.*

When you retrace arcades, fear is the glue that holds them together. The very act of retracing them reinforces the fear of doing something wrong, something that would veer away from the traditional, something that would cause censure—real or imaginary—from an outside source.

Pulling these arcades away from one another gives you freedom of movement, thought, and action, and allows you more spontaneity in all your relationships. It urges you to take risks rather than to cling to the known and familiar.

Third, as you make the arcades, expand them rather than allowing them to curve back toward themselves. The latter is called a *rein-in stroke* (*m n n*) and will cause you to do exactly that with your self-expression. Breathe into your *M M m* . Give it life. Give it freedom. Give it the ability to move.

Fourth, to complete your *M M m* in a magnificent way, have the arcades gradually diminish in size, cascading downward (*m*). This simple action will support your willingness to trust and allow you to let go of any need to control.

Think of the *M M m* as a waterfall—fluid, gently moving and flowing. Hebrew Cabalistic tradition says that from the letter *mem* came the water element. If you're Jewish, or even if you're not and that helps you remember, think of that when you draw your *M M m*'s.

Uppercase *M* (arcaded)

Considerations:

1. Introduce this letter with a gently curved stroke—the humor flourish—with two arcades written in a cascading fashion, the first one higher than the second.

2. Pull the arcades apart, creating a *v* shape close to the baseline.

3. Have the arcades flow downward.

4. End with a gentle garland stroke at the baseline.

Uppercase *M* (pointed)

Considerations:

1. Begin at the baseline with a gentle introductory garland, the Lincoln foot.

2. Create points in the upper zone.

3. Come to the baseline, creating a slight garland in the middle at the baseline.

4. Have the second point lower than the first, in a cascading motion to the right.

5. End with a gentle garland stroke at the baseline.

Lowercase *m*

Considerations:

1. Beginning at the baseline, draw a miniature of the uppercase with three arcades, pulling them apart at the baseline.

2. Have them cascade gently downward.

Personal Application of the Letter *M M m*

If you are compelled to control conversations, negotiations, outcomes, and relationships rather than accepting and evaluating input and letting circumstances unfold naturally, the letter *M M m* can be a breath of fresh air not only for you, but for everyone around you. By practicing this letter until it becomes a natural extension of yourself, a certain ease of spirit will occur, a perceptible lightness that flows from getting out of your own way. If you want to experience a certain grace in relationships as perhaps you never have, accept the challenge of practicing the letter *M M m*.

$\mathcal{N} \, \mathcal{N} \, \mathcal{m}$: The Letter of Friendship

The letter $\mathcal{N} \, \mathcal{n}$ is literally half an $\mathcal{M} \, \mathcal{m}$. It indicates how well we relate to persons one on one. It is the letter of friendship—the most perfect of all relationships, for true friendship is free of expectations of any kind.

Whereas the $\mathcal{M}$ has two arcades, the $\mathcal{N}$ has but one. If you have difficulties relating to people individually, study your $\mathcal{N} \, \mathcal{n}$, and change it slowly. Use the $\mathcal{N}$ now and again to add the element of a light, playful heart. As with the $\mathcal{M} \, \mathcal{M} \, \mathcal{n}$, allow the $\mathcal{N}$ to expand rather than contract, go gently downward, and end softly.

Uppercase $\mathcal{N}$

Considerations:

1. Same as for $\mathcal{M}$, less one arcade.

Uppercase $\mathcal{N}$

Considerations:

1. Introduce this letter with a gentle curve beginning at the baseline, extending gracefully to the top of the upper zone.

2. Drop to the baseline, creating a vertical mid-bar.

3. End with a bit of a slight curve off to the right, ending at the top of the upper zone.

Lowercase $\mathcal{n}$

Considerations:

1. Same as for $\mathcal{m}$, less one arcade.

Personal Application of the Letter $\mathcal{N} \, \mathcal{N} \, \mathcal{n}$

Drawn healthily, this simple letter brings a naturalness and ease into your personal relationships, allowing them to blossom sincerely, without compulsion. If you select the $N\,\mathcal{N}\,\mathcal{n}$ as one of the letters you want to practice, alternate the uppercase, using one and then the other, as each brings in a different energy and attitude. If your profession is one in which you regularly see people on a one-on-one basis, the $N\,\mathcal{N}\,\mathcal{n}$ will positively facilitate your interactions.

$H\,h$: The Letter of Dynamic Self-expression

The letter $H\,h$ is very nearly my favorite letter. I have practiced it every day for over twenty years. I love this letter. It is magnificent, outstanding, and totally awesome. In handwriting, the $H\,h$ represents the willingness to express fully in everyday life what our dreams are for a better world, without holding back—ever.

That doesn't mean doing what others think we should be doing, or doing what's safe and acceptable, or staying in a lucrative career only because it puts butter on our bread. It means doing what we really want to do in the world every day, all day, and speaking about it openly, with the zeal of an evangelist and the wide-eyed innocence of a child. That is the $H\,h$ enlivened, electrified, and expressed. I know this letter intimately.

You might notice, just for fun, that the lowercase h and y are very nearly the same turned on their heads. Go back to the meaning of the $y\,y$ and you will see how they are related on a deeper level.

This letter, along with the f, has caused more rapid personal transformation in persons I have worked with than almost any other letter change. If yours does not resemble the ones here, and you are experiencing frustration or disappointment with your life path, you might want to consider playing with the $H\,h$. It is truly a miracle letter.

Uppercase *H*

Considerations:

1. Starting at the top of the upper zone, draw a firm downstroke to the baseline, the "I am!" stroke.

2. Pick up the pen and do the second firm downstroke.

3. Keeping the pen on the paper, reach back to the left, creating a gentle loop that states "Nothing can stop me!"

4. Finish with a vigorous stroke in a rightward direction.

Lowercase *h*

Considerations:

1. Always begin at the baseline.

2. Make a stroke into the upper zone, creating a moderate-size loop, between 2 and 2½ times as tall as the midzone, a miniature letter *l*, reflecting our basic spiritual nature.

3. Come to the baseline, gently pull away from the loop, and create a *v* at the baseline as you shape an expanded arcade.

4. End with a subtle garland off to the right. Dramatic and clear—what else can you ask for? It's all there in one letter!

Personal Application of the Letter *H h*

Although it would be beneficial for anyone to practice this power-packed letter, it is especially designed for those who as yet have been unable to define clearly what their life path is and are demanding to know so they can get on with it.

Practicing the letter *H h* consistently and with purpose will open doors, transform obstacles into opportunities, allow hidden gifts to surface, and create openings you never dreamed of. What it will *not* do is allow you to sit back and just watch life go by. Oh no! It will throw you into the mix as an active participant in your own life. This is an action letter, one of forward movement and commitment. You have been forewarned!

One of my students, a strong-willed, well-known professional, had been in her present job for more than twenty years when she came to study with me. Monique was doing exceptionally well in her position, receiving accolades and awards from all over, yet she had become restless, knowing that "there was something more." She had reached a dead end. She was bored—a common dilemma.

On top of that, she came from a very conservative part of the world. So conservative, in fact, that each time she would fly home after a weekend class, she was assailed with questions. "Handwriting? Why would an adult study handwriting? In California? You know how strange those Californians are . . . cults everywhere." Because she was known for her quick temper and wit, many comments were whispered behind her back.

Part of the course curriculum is that each student adopt specific handwriting changes themselves in order to experience personally the effects of this technology. After the first weekend class Monique took on several writing changes and her life began to unfold quickly in the most surprising ways. Her temper began to disappear. Her observation? "I just don't get mad anymore; no buttons to push. I find it most amazing." She had begun to let people be as they were with no bones to pick, nothing to prove, and no one to change. She had begun to speak calmly—from fact, not opinion. Because she had released her judgments, no one could ruffle her feathers anymore. She became approachable.

A month later, in our second weekend, the class assignment was for each student to integrate a healthy $H h$ in daily writing. Driven and determined by nature, Monique took it on with zeal. Within a week she called and left a message on my voice mail: "Vimala, I *hate* this letter! I *hate* the Hh! Just *hate* it!" Had her temper returned? As her message continued I received my answer. She started to laugh. "Vimala, this is *so hard*. My hand just won't do what I want it to do! I've written *pages* of h's and most of them look like dirt. What the heck is going on?!"

Since we had devoted over two hours of class time to this mischievous letter I realized she was framing her frustration with a rhetorical question.

To shorten a long story, Monique ended up quitting her high-profile job and selling her home, which she had just had redecorated. She packed up everything she owned and moved away from all that was familiar to a setting in which she felt alive and renewed, beginning life anew in an entirely different career. She has never been happier, never laughed as much, never felt freer, and whenever doubts begin to creep in, as she tells me, "I write pages of Hh's to reassure myself. Now that I'm not fighting them anymore they settle me down, calm my spirit, and put me back on track. Darned letter. I'm coming to love it."

Chapter 8
THE FAMILY OF INSIGHT

$\mathcal{L} \mathcal{L} l, \ E \mathcal{E} \varepsilon, \ I i, \ J \mathcal{J} j$

$L \mathcal{L} l$: The Letter of Innate Spirituality

In the language of the alphabetician, this luscious letter represents the degree of spiritual evolution we were born with and how much attention we have put into developing it in our lifetime. Essentially, it reflects our degree of spiritual maturity.

The letter $\mathcal{L} L l$ is of particular assistance for the person who is determined to find out what makes her tick on a deep inner level. This letter does not relate to our personality, but to that part of us that does not change and cannot be altered, that part of us that is an echo of the Universal Soul commonly called Spirit. It is not dependent on a belief system to exist. It is one of the most essential letters to keep in balance. Practicing this letter in a healthy manner can cause major breakthroughs in your basic approach to life.

Uppercase L

Considerations:

1. Draw a firm downstroke to the baseline and create a right angle.

Uppercase $\mathcal{L}$

Considerations:

1. Begin with a gentle arc in the upper zone.
2. Create a gentle curved stroke to the baseline.
3. Draw a small loop at the baseline.
4. End with a gentle horizontal curve to the right.

Feel the energy contained within each uppercase $\mathcal{L}L$, and decide for yourself which to use, or alternate them.

Lowercase l

Considerations:

1. Always begin at the baseline.
2. Make a stroke into the upper zone, creating a moderate-size loop as the stroke descends to the baseline.
3. Finish at the baseline with a gentle garland to the right.

Personal Application of the Letter $\mathcal{L}L l$

If you are working on awakening to the essence of who you really are, especially your basic spiritual nature, it certainly wouldn't hurt to put consistent daily practice of the letter $\mathcal{L}L l$ at the top of your list. By spiritual nature I am not referring to a belief system or a religion. I am referring to the essential You that is a part of all of humanity. By refining and developing this part of yourself, self-awareness occurs with amazing speed.

So often we sacrifice our integrity by shaping our decisions and behavior around what we feel others will think about us, rather than being true to ourselves: just one little gossipy story, just one little lie, just one little omission, just one little exaggeration. If these "one littles" are a part of your life and you don't want them to be, by practicing the letter $L \mathcal{L} \ell$ consistently you will think twice, maybe three times, before you fall into that habit. The letter $L \mathcal{L} \ell$ encourages you to choose from Spirit. Keep Miracle Notes; you may be astounded.

$E \; \mathcal{E} \; \varrho \; \varepsilon$: The Letter of Tolerance

The letter $E \; \mathcal{E} \varrho \varepsilon$ has a history almost as far back as recorded language. Even the Egyptian Hieratic alphabet* had the letter, although it was turned on its side: ⊓ .

Alphabetically it represents our willingness to listen to others and to exhibit compassion and understanding toward those with an unfamiliar or differing outlook, belief system, or heritage. It is the letter of listening without bias. It is the letter of tolerance.

If you find yourself regularly using such phrases as "I think," or "I believe," or the word "should," you probably view the world as headed for perdition, given the current state of affairs, and easily point fingers—away from yourself. You may also suggest, "If only" this and "If only" that, and find it impossible to have a productive dialogue with someone who doesn't agree with you.

If any of this fits and you'd like it to change, begin practicing this letter today. Then, as the days and weeks go by, stand back and watch your heart open up, your views become gentler around the edges, your understanding take root, and your need to tell others "how it is" diminish considerably, perhaps even disappear. As this happens your ulcers might begin to heal, your blood pressure might come down,

---

*Egyptian business or administrative script that superseded hieroglyphs.

and who knows—someone you least suspect may give you flowers for your birthday.

Uppercase E

Considerations:

1. Draw a firm downstroke to the baseline.
2. Create a right angle.
3. Draw a top horizontal stroke, left to right.
4. Draw another horizontal stroke at the top of the midzone, a bit shorter than the first one, touching the initial downstroke and finishing off in a rightward direction.

Uppercase Ɛ

Considerations:

1. Draw a simple reverse number 3, occupying the upper and midzone.
2. Simplicity: no loops, no introductory strokes, no angles.

The Lowercase Teardrop e

Considerations:

1. Begin with a garland at the baseline.
2. Ascend to the top of the midzone.
3. Create a moderate loop as you come back to the baseline.
4. Make sure this loop is expanded, not closed.
5. End with a gentle garland to the right.

The Lowercase Epsilon ε

Considerations:

1. Draw a reverse number 3, occupying the midzone.
2. It may begin with an introductory stroke ℰ.
3. Simplicity: no loops, no angles.

Personal Application of the Letter *E Ɛ ℓ ε*

If your *E ℓ*'s are dramatically different from the healthy ones shown here, practicing them may be quite a challenge. Their openness and freedom of movement invite your mind to react in like manner toward the beliefs and behavior of others. It is a letter of immense tolerance, a clear pathway to self-acceptance and understanding. The epsilon *Ɛ ε* also brings out your creative nature, particularly your writing ability. Combined with the lowercase epsilon r (*ℰ*), so-called because it resembles the *ε*, your novel is well on its way to becoming a reality.

I ι : The Letter of Clear Perception

Alphabetically, the letter *I ι* has several meanings in the English language because it has more than one manifestation. It is not only an upper- and lowercase letter, it also doubles as a capitalized pronoun representing "me." It is both a letter and an identity. To make the distinction clear, I will abbreviate the Personal Pronoun *I* and refer to it as the PPI.

The letter *I ι* that is not the personal pronoun reflects the degree to which we are present to circumstances that involve us personally. It answers the question, "Am I seeing this clearly, or am I exaggerating what I see?"

The shape of the lowercase *ι* stem reflects how clearly and impersonally we interpret circumstances in which we are personally involved, and to what degree we enlarge upon them. The placement of the *ι* dot tells us where the attention is focused.

Look at the page of writing you filled when you first began reading this book. Where did you place your *ι* dots? If the focus of your attention is on your vacation two months down the road, the dots will be off to the right. If you are still ruminating about the business deal that blew up three weeks ago, your i dots will be to the left. If you are right here, right now, your i dots will be directly over the i stem.

If your thoughts vacillate, however, between your vacation-to-be, the business-deal-gone-bad, what you are going to have for lunch, and your upcoming weekend plans, your i dots will be all over the place. If i dots are frequently missing, it can mean one of several things. In medium to large writing it reflects a person who sees the "big picture" and leaves the details to someone else. In small to tiny writing—especially when combined with angles—it represents people with an extraordinarily keen intelligence. They become completely absorbed in the minute details of the task at hand and their focused, analytical minds simply aren't paying attention to anything else—including i dots. Nikola Tesla is a shining example of this habit. For a sample of his writing, turn to Chapter Three, number sixteen, Angles and Curves.

The Personal Pronoun I

The vertical line is one of the most ancient and simplest of human signs, yet it becomes an anamoly in the English language for it represents the stately uppercase I, which doubles as the personal pronoun I (PPI). English, by the way, is the only language that capitalizes the pronoun for oneself. Other languages capitalize the pronoun representing *you*: German, Spanish, and Russian, to name a few.

Your uppercase I may look slightly different from your PPI, yet for some writers both I's are very nearly identical; either way is fine. Although the meaning of the ordinary uppercase I is merely an extension of the lowercase, the meaning of the PPI is filled with so

126

many nuances and deeply embedded core attitudes that an entire book has been written on this intriguing letter.*

For our purposes, I will say that if you notice in your overall writing that although your slant is consistent, your PPI tilts to the left, straighten it up to align with the prevailing slant.

Uppercase I (not the PPI)

Considerations:

1. Begin at the top of the upper zone, creating a firm downstroke to the baseline.

2. Draw two firm crossbars, bottom and top, slightly shorter than the length of the downstroke.

3. Tilt the top crossbar slightly upward. This brings in the attitude of possibility and forward movement.

Lowercase i

Considerations:

1. Begin with a garland.

2. Ascend to the top of the midzone.

3. As you come back to the baseline, retrace the upstroke.

4. End with a gentle garland to the right.

5. Place the dot directly over the stem, as close as possible without touching it.

Personal Application of the Letter $I\,i$

As with several other letters, the letter $I\,i$ is intimately involved with the writer's personal image. It is extremely important to keep

---

You & Your Private I by Jane Nugent Green. St. Paul, MN: Tyestring Productions, 1988.

this letter in balance, avoiding all the traps mentioned above. If you have trouble standing your ground, and gently but firmly claiming your space, begin practicing this letter religiously—especially the uppercase. Write lines of it every day, pages if you feel like it. Clients who have faithfully worked with this letter tell me that even their physical posture became straighter!

The stabilizing factor to the shape of this fabulous letter is the vertical stroke, which is called the "I am" stroke. It occurs in many uppercase letters, but not with the same importance as in the letter I, for in the English language this letter is a personal statement. Make it count.

Along with the letter $I\ i$, you might also begin practicing the letters $A\ a$ and $T\ \mathcal{I}$, since these three letters lend support and balance to one another.

$J\ \mathcal{J}\ j$: The Letter of Intuition

The letter $J\ \mathcal{J}\ j$ is the newest addition to our English dictionary, having finally been given a place there at the turn of the ninteenth century. For centuries it has been considered a mere consonantal form of the letter $I\ i$, not a letter in its own right. Even the illustrious Dr. Samuel Johnson in his *Dictionary of the English Language* (1755) did not give it a chapter all its own, but included it as a variation of the letter $I\ i$.

Like the letter $I\ i$, the letter $J\ \mathcal{J}\ j$ indicates to what degree we are present to circumstances when we are personally involved, but it goes beyond that and drops into the lower zone, tapping into what is often called gut instinct. The letter $J\ \mathcal{J}\ j$, then, represents our instinctual insight.

The $\cup$ $\mathcal{G}$ j reflects how we feel about something or someone, not emotionally, but that kind of feeling-knowing triggered by the sixth sense we all possess, called by such names as insight, intuition, psychic ability, or hunches. The $\cup$ $\mathcal{G}$ j represents instinctual knowledge—that gut feeling that we *know* is correct even though we may set it aside as implausible—and later wish we had "listened."

Uppercase $\cup$

Considerations:

1. Create a firm downstroke to the baseline, ending in a garland shape to the left that ends in an upward direction.

2. No angles, no loops.

Uppercase $\mathcal{G}$

Considerations:

1. Begin at the baseline, creating a generous leftward loop in the upper zone.

2. Drop firmly into the lower zone, creating a moderate loop to the left of the descender, narrower than the upper loop.

3. Return to the baseline and finish by crossing over the beginning stroke at the baseline in a rightward direction.

Lowercase j

Considerations:

1. Begin at the baseline with a gentle upstroke.

2. Drop firmly into the lower zone, creating a moderate loop to the left of the descender, 2 to 2½ times as long as the height of the midzone.

3. Return to the baseline and end in a rightward direction.

4. Place a dot directly over the stem. No circle, star, or other decoration. A dot.

Personal Application of the Letter J *J j*

If you are wary about following your hunches, then later criticize yourself for not having done so, this may be the letter for you to begin practicing. It will give you permission to act on the knowledge that logic is not the only way to reach conclusions or make decisions. It will remove any overly vigilant mental guardedness and give you direct access to your intuitive nature. It will encourage you to act on your gut feelings. Try it on for size. You may find yourself smiling a lot!

Chapter 9
THE FAMILY OF APPLIED CREATIVITY

Ff, Rrr, Ss

F*f* : The Letter of Using One's Talents
in Service to Others

The letter F*f* is one of the most fascinating of all the letters in our alphabet. It is also one of the most challenging to alter because it shifts so many of our thought habits simultaneously. It reflects a consciousness that is grounded, creative, organized, expressive, and trusting, all in one package. It is the only lowercase letter to occupy all three zones: upper, mid, and lower. It reflects our willingness to give our unique gifts the breath of creative expression in service to others.

Because this letter is so intertwined with being fully involved in your own creative process, I am going to list a few *f*'s you do not want to do. I put them here because they are so common, and so backward-moving.

I call this The Secretary's *f* . The top loop, the area of our own unique creativity, is missing. It is often the "f" of someone who does someone else's work quite well and thoroughly, but has not opened the treasure chest of her own ideas and put them in motion. I say *her* because it occurs almost exclusively in women's handwriting. I call it The Secretary's *f* because it carries the consciousness not of service, but of servitude.

This is the self-sabotage *f*. It is so called because the lower loop is reversed. The lower zone is the area of action, relationship, and forward movement. When the loop is reversed in this particular letter it shifts life, projects, and relationships into a well-oiled reverse.

Persons who write this *f* consistently may find themselves with a lifelong pattern of difficulty where commitment and completion are concerned. Plans will progress to a certain point, then everything falls apart. The answer to "What happened?" is, "On a subconscious level, you set it up that way."

So you will have them in a concise format for review, here are the five parts of the letter *f* and the statement each stroke makes.

1. Begin at the baseline. "I am grounded."

2. Loop in the upper zone. "I fully acknowledge my creative gifts."

3. Lower loop. "I am willing to be in action with my gifts, shaping them into a tangible form that will uplift humanity in some way."

4. Tie stroke. "Nothing will stop me."

5. Final garland at the baseline, driving off to the right. "I've given it my all; the results are in God's hands."

Uppercase *F*

Considerations:

1. From the top of the upper zone, create a firm downstroke to the baseline.

2. Place one horizontal bar on the top and one in the middle.

3. Tilt the horizontal strokes sightly upward.

Lowercase *f*

Considerations:

1. Begin with a gentle garland at the baseline.

2. Create an upper loop of moderate height and width.

3. Drop into the lower zone, then bring the stroke back up on the right side of the descender.

4. Create a loop that is slightly longer and slightly wider than the upper loop.

5. As you reach the baseline, go to the left of the initial down-stroke, creating a tie stroke as you come forward again.

6. Finish in a rightward direction, on the baseline.

Personal Application of the Letter *Ff*

Everyone is creative in some way, everyone is special in some way, and everyone came into life with a very specific purpose. Everyone. The letter *Ff* represents acknowledging our gifts, expressing them for the benefit of society, and at the same time being totally unat-tached to how they are manifested.

If you could use a little more of this attitude in your life, embrace the letter *Ff* as your letter for forty days and see what happens. The effects of this letter are so quick that you may find yourself adding pages rather than paragraphs to your Miracle Notes.

R r r: The Letter of Innate Creativity

The letter *R r r* is the letter of innate creativity. Like your unique-ness and mine, *R r r*'s come in a variety of shapes and sizes, and their energy lives deep within. When you shape this letter, keep in mind its different aspects and you can begin to activate, awaken, or refine them in your own life.

Uppercase R

Considerations:

1. Draw a firm downstroke to the baseline.

2. Pick up the pen and draw a rounded arc on the top half of the initial stroke.

3. Keeping pen to paper, finish with a slightly curved stroke, reaching forward on the baseline.

Lowercase r (slightly sloping, flattopped)

Considerations:

1. Begin at the baseline with a gentle upstroke, making a tiny loop at the top of the midzone.

2. Draw a slightly tipped horizontal stroke.

3. Create an expanded formation, return to the baseline, and finish with a gentle garland to the right.

Modify this r slightly by making a tiny loop as the upstroke changes directions (r), and your creative writer will have no choice but to bubble enthusiastically to the surface.

Lowercase r

Considerations:

1. Beginning at the baseline, draw an upstroke, then a firm vertical downstroke to the baseline.

2. Pulling away from the downstroke, create an arch-shaped finish at the top of the midzone.

This r is especially helpful for the scientist, the engineer, the physics teacher, the person whose job it is to bring abstract concepts down to a practical level.

It creates a working relationship between the upper zone, the baseline, and a rightward direction. It joins the energies of the mind, everyday reality, and future application. Draw a few. See how they feel.

Personal Application of the Letter R ₁₌

The letter R ₁₌ acts like a spade, unearthing talents that have been buried for some time, many of which you may not even be aware of. If you have a strong inkling that you have specific creative abilities, given what you loved to do when you were a young child, begin writing the R ₁₌ purposefully and consistently, then take notes about what ideas begin to pop into your mind.

If your novel, symphony, or painting just won't take shape, combine the use of this lowercase ₌ and ₌ with the figure-eight ₈ and watch the pieces come together with amazing speed. My advice? Stand back—genius at work!

S s : The Letter of Balance

The letter S s is a letter of great dignity. It represents what most of us are striving for in all areas of our life: *balance,* i.e., reducing the stress level in our lives. It has to do with juggling play, work, prayer, relationships, speaking, dancing, and laughing, each in balance with the other as they add fullness and joy to life, with no extremes anywhere. Its message could easily be, "Keep those apples in the air gently now, gently."

The message of the letter S s is "neither too much nor too little." Balance play with work, becoming neither a workaholic nor a playaholic. As much as you talk, be silent. As much as you take, give. As much as you give, be willing to receive. Balance. Balance: like a ballerina *en pointe,* graciously poised for the next step, ready to turn in any direction.

The attitudes emphasized by the old-fashioned s's we were taught in elementary school were grasping, tightness, and a me-first attitude. The uppercase was tightly drawn with a knot at the top and a slash at the bottom ($\mathcal{S}$). The lowercase was pointed at the top and tied shut with a slash ($\mathcal{A}$). Not a wise choice to make if stress is paramount in your life!

If you want to experience the difference between the emphases of these two s's, write a few lines of the ones you learned in school, then write a few lines of these: $\mathcal{S}$ $\mathcal{S}$ $\mathcal{S}$ $\mathcal{S}$ s s s s . Feel the difference for yourself.

Many clients have told me that when they practice writing this $\mathcal{S}$ s they feel their shoulders relax, tension releases in their neck, and their grip on the pen lightens up as well.

Because balance is vital in handling stress and conflict, the letter $\mathcal{S}$ s is a key letter for you if you are constantly being stretched beyond what is comfortable in attempting to handle your professional, social, and family life.

While we're on the subject of stress, this is a stroke you may want to incorporate in your writing—or your doodling. It will immediately lower blood pressure, slow down breathing, allay anxiety, and reduce mental tension. I call it Miles of Lace.

I share this writing stroke in workshops I offer for health professionals, and continue to receive many gratifying stories from them. Psychiatric technicians, nurses, and doctors all over the country tell me they encourage their patients to sit once a day and write only the

Miles of Lace for pages and pages. The results have been spectacular, beautiful, heartwarming, lovely to see, unbelievable, "brings tears to the eyes," and such a blessing . . . all phrases used in the letters I have received.

Because it has a reverse, slowing-down effect, be sure not to use it as your uppercase *L*.

Uppercase *S*

Considerations:

1. Begin at the top of the upper zone as though shaping a c.

2. At the top of the midzone, reverse the stroke and create a reverse c between the midzone and the baseline.

3. Finish at the baseline with a gently curved loop to the right.

Lowercase *s*

Considerations:

1. A miniature of the uppercase, occupying the midzone.

Personal Application of the Letter *S s*

If you notice that what undermines you is a tendency toward extremes, or juggling too many things at once, or both, begin practicing this *S s* today. Play with it, make it fun, incorporate it into your daily writing, and feel your energy drawn back to center instead of leaning over too far or running around without direction. A most astonishing letter.

Chapter 10
THE FAMILY OF STATUS

Tt, Kk, Bb

Tt: The Letter of Status

The statuesque letter Tt makes quite a statement. This is as it should be, for it represents the attitude we have toward our profession, toward the image we present in the world, and how tall we are willing to stand. It is the letter of self-worth and self-esteem.

If you remember, its cousin the Dd reflects who we are in the world. The Tt is a standard for what we do: our life work, our profession, and the energy, determination, and purpose we are willing to invest in that.

This majestic letter deals with the willingness to excel, to stand nobly with head held high, refusing to drag mediocrity behind us as our banner. It has two parts, the stem and the crossbar, which engage in a dance. When they are dynamically drawn their posture is erect, their arms outstretched, and their momentum charged with forward movement.

Write this letter with firm purpose and clear intention. Let your pen dance with it. Make it clear and distinct. Above all, make sure there is no loop in the vertical stem. A loop here indicates sensitivity about our role or profession; it can hold you back from experiencing a sense of pride in what you do. Place the crossbar on top of the stem—not a hair's breadth down from the top, but right on top. This indicates how far you are willing to stretch to reach your goals. As the T crossbar slips down the stem, so does your commitment to achieve. The ones we were taught in school with the crossbars placed midway down the stem reinforced mediocrity.

The stem is vertical and occupies the mid- and upper zones in both the upper- and lowercase formations. The shape of the crossbar is key because it is your *willpower stroke*—the one that sets your goals and infuses them with the willingness to stretch to reach them.

The letter T T encapsulates your sense of purpose and your self-esteem more succinctly than any other stroke combination, for these two qualities proclaim the degree of energy you are willing to invest in your dreams, your projects, and your life.

Uppercase T

Considerations:

1. Draw a firm downstroke to the baseline.

2. Pick up the pen. Place a firm crossbar tilted sightly upward on top of the initial stroke.

3. Have half the crossbar on each side of the stem, tilted slightly upward.

4. Make sure the crossbar rests on top of the stem and does not fly off or slide down.

Lowercase T

Considerations:

1. Begin with a garland at the baseline, then ascend to the top of the upper zone.

2. As you begin the descent to the baseline, retrace the upstroke exactly. Do not put a loop in it.

3. Finish with a garland at the baseline.

4. Pick up your pen.

5. Place a firmly drawn crossbar on top of the stem, with half the crossbar on each side of the stem.

6. As with the uppercase, make sure the crossbar rests on top of the stem and does not fly off or slide down.

Personal Application of the Letter *T T*

If important goals seem beyond your reach and your self-esteem needs a little boost, this letter will sustain and support you. The statement of a *T T* powerfully drawn echoes the spirit of a person who is determined, driven, and enthusiastic, one who strives to set and reach goals far beyond the ordinary human being. It is the statement of a person who is fully alive. If this resonates with who you know yourself to be, claim this letter as your own, pick up your pen, and begin today to write it.

Th th Ligature: The Letter of Flexibility

A ligature is a combination of two letters, the second of which is created from a part of the first. Review the description of this mighty stroke combination under eighteen in Chapter Three and incorporate this letter frequently in your writing. Be careful, however, to avoid the counterproductive bowl stroke: *th*.

Personal Application of the *Th*

This uppercase ligature not only brings in fluidity; as a crossbar the *umbrella-like stroke* adds the attitude of self-discipline. If you feel this quality would help you reach any goals you have set—exercising regularly, watching your food intake, giving up smoking—this is the letter to begin practicing rigorously. You will feel its effect right away.

To further instill the quality of self-discipline you might consider making a curved crossbar not only on the *Th* ligature, but on the plain *T* as well.

Personal Application of the *th*

If you work or live with persons with whom you frequently do not see eye to eye on important matters, begin to incorporate this letter into your writing; it will make a beautiful difference. If one of these persons is a lover, a spouse, or a child, it will be especially valuable because it will bring the quality of lightness into your discussions.

The gentle *th* will have you listen from a soft place within rather than argue or stop people short when they are speaking; it will open a place inside you that may be unfamiliar yet friendly, like someone you have just met and like instantly. It will help you remain sincerely open to ideas, input, and views contrary to your own. It will bless all your relationships with a sense of openness and willingness to create solutions that work equally well for everyone involved. If this is an alluring concept, use this *Th* as well.

K k : The Letter of Handling Authority

This letter *K k* may look strange to you if you are accustomed to using the outdated one with loop and buckle. "It's printed" you may say. And I would reply, yes it is. This is one letter that is balanced and healthy when it is printed in both its uppercase and lowercase form.

The circular shape that resembles the beginning of an uppercase *R* is called a buckle; it is also the rounded shape in the old-fashioned *k*. Because the letter *K k* reflects the writer's attitude toward authority, this shape is the origin of the phrase "buckle under," for it implies that in order to be respected, we must give up what we want and acquiesce to another's wishes. In other words, "Just do what you're told."

Written in an unbalanced manner, the letter *K k* also can reflect an underlying attitude of rebelliousness. Writers of a healthily drawn letter *K k* can do what is called for, depending on the circumstances, with neither the need to rebel nor the compulsion to hand their power away and go belly-up. Balanced and respectful, the *K k* is a stately letter.

Uppercase *K*

Considerations:

1. Beginning at the top of the upper zone, draw a firm downstroke to the baseline.

2. Pick up the pen.

3. Place a *v* sideways on the first stroke, beginning at the top of the upper zone, finishing at the baseline.

Lowercase *k*

Considerations:

1. A miniature of the uppercase, with the stem the same height as the uppercase.

2. Make the top of the sideways *v* no higher than the top of the midzone.

Personal Application of the Letter *K k*

If you have created a pattern in your life of challenging everyone and everything to your own detriment, the healthy *K k* can alert you to those times when rebelling may not be necessary or useful, or produce the results you want.

The downstroke states your presence and authority. The sideways *v* invites you to make decisions, not in a defensive manner, but carefully, evaluating all available choices. It gives you time to pause and consider rather than simply react. If you find yourself being described here, it may be an adventure for you to take off that suit of armor, throw down your sword, and accept the challenge extended by this grand letter.

$B\ b$: The Letter of Spirit-centered Business

This is a power-packed letter. Well drawn, it is fluid, clear, and distinct. The $B\ b$ represents bringing Spirit into business. It extends an invitation for the most highly principled part of you to flow into all matters dealing with business from a practical, win-win perspective.

A healthy $B\ b$ allows no room for manipulation, greed, or hidden agendas. Balanced, expanded, and clear, it emphasizes cooperation rather than competition, excellence rather than settling for anything less, with the goal of having everyone involved be the winner. Quite a letter.

Uppercase B

Considerations:

1. Beginning at the top of the upper zone, draw a firm downstroke to the baseline.
2. Pick up the pen.
3. Create two rightward arcs, the top smaller than the bottom.
4. Make sure they are closed at the top and bottom.
5. Finish with a gentle internal loop to the right at the baseline.

Lowercase *b*

Considerations:

1. Beginning at the top of the upper zone, draw a firm down-stroke to the baseline.

2. Pick up the pen.

3. Create an arc to the right, finishing with a gentle internal loop to the right.

4. Make sure the arc is closed.

Personal Application of the Letter *B b*

If you are actively engaged in business of any kind—be it teaching, parenting, publishing, selling cars, or politics—this letter, written consistently in a healthy manner, will support you in creating new, positive, and appropriate ways of looking at and solving long-standing problems from a principle-centered base.

To alter a traditional saying, it will give you the ability to "leave the job cleaner than when you found it." More than that, it can have your legacy in a profession provide others with fresh, enlivening patterns to follow, long after you are gone. The *B b* is truly a letter of the twenty-first century.

Chapter 11
THE FAMILY OF TRUSTING
AND INNER AUTHORITY

C c , X x

C c : The Letter of Complete Trust

As innocuous as this simple letter appears, it is one of the most difficult to alter or tidy up. Especially if it is the initial of your first name,
begin drawing it this way—C—and see what it feels like. Even, if I
may suggest, create a new autograph using this simplified version of
this intensely powerful letter.

Like its brother the letter G g g , who was created from the letter
C c , this awesome letter has multiple meanings. It represents trust
at its deepest level, and our willingness to be vulnerable and free from
judgment of ourselves and others—particularly women authority
figures in our lives.

Any kind of hook, loop, twist, or curl—any decoration at all in
this letter—is a mirror of our negative judgment about another person in our life. And it is our negative judgment, not the person herself, that keeps us connected to her.

In the letter C c , this person is most frequently our mother—
who, if you will notice, echoes out into our lives as any female au-

thority figure. Look around. See for yourself. Forgiveness, compassion, vulnerability, openness, unaffected honesty, and true joy are impossible as long as we hold any negative judgments here. Impossible.

There are two things in life we cannot change: the past and other people. Until we bless the past as it was and everyone in it as they were—including ourselves—and let it all go, we cannot create a peaceful now or a peaceful future.

To help release your negative judgments, keep your C c completely open: free of hooks, loops, and any driving strokes from beneath the baseline. Allow nothing to close it off in the slightest. Draw it as a simple three-quarter circle: clear, open, inviting, and free.

Uppercase C

Considerations:

1. Begin at the top of the upper zone, drawing a clean, uncluttered three-quarter circle open to the right, occupying both the upper and midzone.

2. Allow no hooks, circles, loops, or other decorations.

Lowercase c

Considerations:

1. A miniature of the uppercase, occupying the midzone.

Personal Application of the Letter C c

If being critical is an attitude that has plagued you most of your life, and you find yourself blaming your mother for practically every shortcoming in your personality or relationships, and you would like to be rid of this millstone of judgment, begin practicing the letter C c .

Don't be fooled. It may look like a basic, simple form to write, but when you begin practicing it, you may find it otherwise. I once had a client who was determined to be free of her "mother issues," as she called them. She began practicing the letter C c along with two other handwriting changes with determination and intensity.

After three days she called. "Look, Vimala—I've written over twenty pages of these darned C c's. I've used a Rollerball pen, two kinds of ballpoints in different colors, and even a fountain pen, but that darned hook still keeps showing up. What's going on?!" The answer became transparent as she spoke, and we both began to laugh. With the energy still rolling, she finished, "You don't suppose it's judgments I'm holding on to about my mother, do you?" Then we *really* laughed.

X x : The Letter of Inner Authority

Stop a minute. Ask yourself this question: "Where have I seen this letter before?" If you write hugs and kisses at the bottom of notes, this magical letter represents the kisses. If you are illiterate, this telling letter becomes your identity when you are asked to sign a document. No one will ask you to use a Q, L, E, or M as your signature, no matter how regal these letters may be. No. You will be asked to sign your name using the letter X x .

Essentially, the letter X x represents your inner authority—that part of you that represents your exclusivity on this planet, your stance, your solidity, your presence. With four *v*'s joining in the center, it becomes a visual representation of decisions that come from thoughts ($\vee$), feelings ($\wedge$), the past ($\rangle$), the future ($\langle$), and meeting in the heart ($\times$).

Alphabetically the letter $\times$ x has a lengthy history around the globe. In the Germanic runes the letter that is shaped like the $\times$ x is called *gebo*, representing a partnership of self with Self, a definition valid today.

$\times$ x also stands for the unknown, implying the element of mystery. It is the letter the Romans used to designate the number ten, one of the most highly evolved and fundamental numbers in the science of mathematics and the greatest number in Cabalistic and Pythagorean traditions.

Sadly, we have few commonly used words that begin with this eloquent letter, yet quite a few that have the prefix *ex-*, so we do get to write it now and again.

These three facts are vital to remember:

1. The letter $\times$ x represents a solid stance, with four *v*'s connected in the center. If you remember, the letter V v represents making choices that are both self-referred and discriminating.

2. Whenever you write the letter $\times$ x , do not connect it to the letter on the left or the letter on the right. At all times leave this power letter freestanding.

3. Do not introduce, include within, or end this letter with any kind of a curved shape. It is simply four *V*'s connected in the center.

Uppercase $\times$

Considerations:

1. Begin at the top of the upper zone by drawing a diagonal line from the top right to the lower left, ending at the baseline ∕∠. Pick up the pen.

2. Beginning at the top of the upper zone, draw an intersecting diagonal line from upper left to lower right, ending firmly at the baseline ＼↘.

3. The order of these strokes is important, as you want to finish the letter in a rightward direction.

Lowercase x

Considerations:

1. A miniature of the uppercase, occupying the midzone.

Personal Application of the Letter X x

If you find yourself constantly quoting other people to make a point—whether it be the pope, the president, Ralph Waldo Emerson, or the man next door—instead of stating the fact in your own words from your own personal conviction, I definitely recommend you begin practicing the letter X x . To support you, you might also begin practicing the V v as well, the self-reliant lowercase d, and your autograph, as they are all intimately related.

By incorporating all of these into your writing patterns at one time, a strong sense of self will be enhanced and your need to defend, protest, grumble, or quote will gradually disappear. You will have begun to learn to go inside for answers and trust the ones you find.

Chapter 12
THE Z STANDS ALONE

Z, Ʒ, z, ʒ:
The Letter of Perfect Contentment

Because it has such charm and character, for years I have preferred to call this nurturing letter *zed* rather than simply *zee* because *zed* seems to add such character to it.

The letter Z Ʒ z ʒ is a seasoned letter, the Grandfather Letter of the alphabet, for he looks back at the rest of his alphabetical family from a wise place deep within and is able to say gently, with utter conviction and non-judgment, "My life is whole and complete."

Contentment is the prize of a life well lived. It is the virtue earned by using life's experiences as the catalyst to mellow knowledge into wisdom. That all of life is as it should be, that all of life is unfolding perfectly, that all of life is sacred, capture the essence of the letter Z Ʒ z ʒ.

In 1993 I was commenting on my fondness for the letter Z Ʒ z ʒ, and describing its grandfatherly aspects to the class, when Mordecai—one of my students who is also a scholar of Judaica—informed us that *zayde* means grandfather in Yiddish. As he said this, from somewhere deep inside I heard a chorus cheering loudly with approval. I do love this letter.

Uppercase Z

Considerations:

1. Draw a firm horizontal stroke at the top of the upper zone, from left to right.

2. Now draw a diagonal to the left, through the upper and midzones, ending at the baseline.

3. Finish with a rightward stroke at the baseline.

4. Do not pick up the pen from the moment you begin until the letter is complete.

5. Place a short caliph on the diagonal if you choose ($\mathcal{Z}$).

Uppercase ʒ

Considerations:

1. Beginning at the top of the upper zone, create an arc that is open on the left, occupying the upper zone.

2. Continuing from the top of the midzone, drop into the lower zone, creating a full lower loop.

3. Bring the final stroke up and finish it in a rightward direction at the baseline.

Lowercase z

Considerations:

1. A miniature of the printed uppercase, occupying the midzone.

Lowercase *ʒ*

Considerations:

1. A miniature of the reverse epsilon *ʒ*, occupying both the mid-zone and lower zone.

Personal Application of the Letter Z ʒ z ʒ

If you find yourself complaining all the time, wishing things were different, yet not doing anything about it, or you feel anxious and uncertain about the state of your relationships, your job, or the world at large, practicing the letter Z ʒ z ʒ will allay the fear from which these feelings spring and invite you to confront these enemies with "Enough!" and eventually banish them entirely.

The gift of the letter Z ʒ z ʒ is contentment springing from inner peace, which implies no judgments of any kind, an ease of spirit that comes from the knowledge that the world is unfolding at its own pace and the only thing you're responsible to change is yourself, nothing else, no one else. As you begin practicing the Z ʒ z ʒ be sure to keep daily Miracle Notes, for they soon will be filled with the most extraordinary tales on your journey toward self-transformation.

Part Three

MAKING

CHANGES

Chapter 13
HOW TO PRACTICE YOUR
HANDWRITING CHANGES

If you are tired of being a mystified bystander in your own life and are eager to transform your role to that of a joyfully active, engaged participant, adopting handwriting changes is one of the quickest, surest ways to have this occur.

Again—remember the jigsaw puzzle: One piece of the puzzle is only one piece of the puzzle. In order to see the entire picture, each piece must be considered in relation to the others.

1. To obtain the results you want, you must practice your new handwriting every day, at least twenty minutes a day—longer if possible. The more you write, the sooner you will reach your goal.

2. Sketchbooks work well as practice writing books, since they aren't lined. They're usually easy to find, but if that is not the case where you live, have an inch (about 175 sheets) of unlined paper made into a spiral notebook. Most copy stores can do this for you.

3. Write in the landscape direction with a ballpoint or fountain pen.

4. Choose either two miscellaneous changes (spacing and size, for example) along with three letter changes, or the reverse: two letter changes with three miscellaneous changes.

5. Practice each set of writing changes for forty days without skipping a day.

DAILY PRACTICE

Each day, fill both sides of two sheets of paper with your writing.

• For the letter changes: Write three lines of each letter, upper- and lowercase.

Follow this by writing three lines of words of your choice beginning with that letter.

Follow this by writing three lines of words of your choice with the letter in the middle.

Follow this by writing three lines of words of your choice ending with the letter.

• Fill the remainder of your two pages with writing, using both your new letter changes as well as your other writing changes—such as margins, size, etc.

Do not copy something already written; let your thoughts flow freely from the pen. Be patient with yourself. Write slowly. Remember, you are not re-educating your hand, but your mind. It takes deliberation and time for resistance to diminish and changes to flow.

• Practice your writing changes each day for a minimum of forty days. Attempting too many changes at once can be discouraging. Become aware of attitude shifts as you alter your handwriting and jot them down under Miracle Notes.

DURATION OF WRITING PRACTICE

It takes forty days of consistent practice to instill new habits in the mind. It is no accident that in almost all spiritual traditions forty is not just a casual number; it represents a period of preparation before reaching the intended destination. Forty is the number of transformation.

It is the starting place of not-knowing-how-but-trusting that completion will be achieved. Looking back through history, we can see that we are in quite respectable company, given that the lives of all these personages were profoundly affected again and again by this most astounding number: Gilgamesh, Moses, the Israelites, Elijah, Muhammed, Jalaladdin Rumi, the Sufis, Noah, Jonah, the people of Nineveh, and Jesus. You may know of others.

Practice each set of writing changes for forty days and experience the transformation for yourself. On the day you begin, mark your calendar with forty and go backward from forty to one. In other words, day forty is the day you start, the next day is day thirty-nine, and so on, until you get to day one. Be faithful in keeping Miracle Notes each day; they will be like bread crumbs leading you out of the forest into the light.

Congratulations for taking your life into your own hands. May you claim center stage and create a dazzling future!

GLOSSARY

angle: This is any written formation that has two lines creating a $\vee$ shape. Consistent angles at the baseline indicate an analytical mind. Consistent inverted angles at the top of the midzone or upper zone indicate a vigorously curious mind.

arcade: This stroke resembles an archway. Consistent use of these in writing indicates a person who tends to be protective or paternal. The arcaded writer's mind reasons in a step-by-step manner, and is methodical and deliberate, often rechecking what has been done—just in case. It is not common for this writer to risk or take chances when the outcome is in question.

baseline: This is the imaginary invisible line we draw for our words to sit upon as we write.

bowl stroke: This stroke occurs in a t crossbar that connects itself to the following letter (*th*). It dips down, creating a deep bowl-like shape before it reaches out to the next letter. It represents a lack of direction and few if any goals being acted upon by the writer.

bridge stroke: This is a horizontal stroke usually at the top of the midzone, as in the *w* or *o*.

crossbar: This is the horizontal bar that creates the letter t by intersecting or sitting atop the vertical stem. It represents the writer's willpower. *See* willpower stroke.

curve: Whereas an angle has a point, this stroke is soft and bends. A curved stroke in handwriting can be a garland, arc, loop, or arcade.

detrose loop: Detrose means in a rightward direction. This loop is small, tight, and drawn in a rightward direction. Most often it occurs as an introductory stroke to certain uppercase letters, such as the outdated m n x .

downstroke to the baseline: This stroke begins at the top of the upper zone and comes directly to the baseline. It is also called the "I am" stroke, as it consciously and deliberately affirms our presence and intention.

expanded midzone: This refers to creating horizontal expansion rather than contraction in any letters occupying the midzone, particularly in the letters in the Family of Communication, a, o, d, g, q, and p.

figure-eight g: This letter is written so it resembles the numeral 8. It is one of the most powerful strokes you can use to feed your creative nature, as it opens up your heart and lets the creative juices flow.

garland: This curved stroke looks like a garland, thus its name. It reflects an open hand, with the ability to both give and receive. When appearing consistently in handwriting, it symbolizes a writer who is a people person and whose nature it is to reach out to others. Garlands can occur within letter formations, in connective strokes between letters, or as introductory or ending strokes.

ligature: This letter is a combination of two letters, the second one of which is created from a part of the first one, as in th. Next to the ampersand—$\&$—which is an artistic form of *et* and means *and* in Latin, th is the most commonly used ligature in the English language. A ligature represents a fluid thinker with a flexible attitude, who copes well in stressful situations. *See* bowl stroke.

Lincoln foot: This term refers to the introductory stroke Abraham Lincoln used in his autograph. It is the introductory stroke of the Vimala Alphabet A and M.

loops: These formations occur in all zones. They are always containers; where they occur determines what they contain. A loop in any zone can reinforce either positive or negative attributes. The meaning depends on how it is drawn and in what letter it occurs.

margin: This is the space we leave around the outer edges of our writing. It defines the area we have chosen to occupy in life and delineates the boundaries we have set.

paper direction: Landscape is a way of saying the long way. It looks like this: ☐. Portrait is a way of saying the narrow or traditional, familiar way. It looks like this: ▯.

paraph: This is the final stroke of your autograph.

midzone-retraced strokes: There are two kinds of retraced strokes in the midzone: an *upstroke* as in the letters d, i, and t (it is desirable to retrace them) and a *downstroke* as in the letters m, n, and h (it is not desirable to retrace them).

rein-in stroke: This stroke is named for its movement. It prevents the creative energy from continuing in a forward motion and reins it in. Extremely repressive, the writer of this stroke is kicking the horse and pulling on the reins at the same time. It occurs most often in the letters m, n, h, and r and looks like this: m n h r.

self-sabotage stroke: The most common of these seductive strokes is created by writing the letter f with a reversed lower loop. Because forward-moving energy is retarded by creating a lower loop of this nature, a person who writes this stroke with consistency has great difficulty with commitment and completion.

slant: This term refers to which way the handwriting patterns tend to tilt: to the left, vertical, or to the right.

umbrella stroke: This powerful stroke is the crossbar on the letter t, drawn with a slight curve resembling an umbrella. It represents self-discipline.

upswings: These strokes occur at the end of a word. Because of the way they are shaped, they block forward movement ($\mathcal{U}$).

willpower stroke: This is the $\mathcal{T}$ crossbar. *See* crossbar.

zones: There are three zones in handwriting. The upper zone reflects thoughts, creativity, beliefs, anything that goes on inside the head. The midzone represents everyday life such as bathing the dog, driving the car, shaking hands, etc. The lower zone reflects relationships, movement and activity, endurance, sexuality, and a service-oriented focus.

REFERENCES

Green, Jane Nugent. *You & Your Private I*. St. Paul, Minnesota: Tyestring Productions, 1988.

Hall, Manly P. *Secret Teachings of All Ages*. Los Angeles, California: Philosophical Research Society, 1977.

Rael, Joseph, with Mary Elizabeth Marlow. *Being and Vibration*. Oklahoma: Council Oak Books, 1993.

Rodgers, Vimala. *Change Your Handwriting, Change Your Life*. Berkeley, California: Celestial Arts, 1993.

(Spanish edition) *Cambia tu Escritura para Cambiar tu Vida*. Barcelona, Spain: Ediciones Urano, 1997.

Suetonius. *De Vita Caesarum: Diuus Iulius*. Liber I. Cambridge, Massachusetts: Harvard University Press, Loeb Classical Library. 1995.

INDEX

ABOUT THE AUTHOR

VIMALA RODGERS is an educator, handwriting expert, Master Alphabetician, and peak-performance coach. Drawing from a lifetime of study and research, Rodgers is pioneering the development of technology that focuses on character building and personal transformation through healthy writing. In 1991 she founded the Vimala Rodgers Institute of Integral Handwriting Studies (IIHS) through which to share her findings.

Trained at Stanford University in the psychology of peak performance, Rodgers works with individuals and groups who want to transform their relationships, their world, their future.

Her article "Handwriting and Self-Esteem" was published in the Association for Humanistic Psychology journal *Perspective;* her work had been featured on radio and television, in magazines and newspapers. A well-known motivational speaker, Rodgers has offered presentations for such diverse groups as the Academic Senate at the University of San Francisco; faculty, staff, and students at Stanford University and the Institute of Transpersonal Psychology; and members of Hospital Consortia nationwide.

From its vision that world peace is possible, IIHS is involved in spreading healthy handwriting throughout the global educational community. If this is something that interests you, we'd love to hear from you. Blessings to you on your journey.

Vimala Rodgers

Visit us at:
http://www.iihs.com
vimalpha@iihs.com

176